For my queer family:
I do all this through you who give me strength.

AUTHOR'S NOTE

This is a work of nonfiction. The events and experiences detailed herein have been faithfully rendered as I have remembered them, to the best of my ability. Some names, identities, and circumstances have been changed in order to protect the integrity and/or anonymity of the various individuals involved. Though conversations come from my keen recollection of them, they are not written to represent word-for-word documentation; rather, they have been retold in a way that evokes the real feeling and meaning of what was said, in keeping with the true essence of the mood and spirit of the event. Any commentary pertaining to public figures, institutions, or policies is intended as personal opinion.

MENU

PART 1

PART 2

PART 3

Dinner on Monster Island

Tell your people that this flesh tomb is risen,
Stone slid away,
Where is the body you tried to bury?

—WORMS VIRK, *THE BODY IS A TEMPLE*

Salvation

The year 1993. That's when it happens. Two months after your twelfth birthday. It's a sweaty afternoon. This day which blisters with possibility. This day you learn that there are demons inside of you.

You're on your way home from school. You know something is wrong the minute you get off the bus. Your mother waits at the bus stop, teary-eyed. Your relationship has become monosyllabic. But the way she looks at you through the tears fills you with unease, so you ask.

What's wrong?

It is when she smiles that something inside you unravels. You realize hers are happy tears. But her smile is vacant. Placid. A Stepford Wife smile. The tears fall but there is nothing behind them. She's a mannequin crying on command.

You don't have language for this yet.

She grabs you, holds you tight: *Nana has been saved!*

———◆———

Till that point, Nana, my grandmother, had been a devout Catholic her whole life. That she converted to Pentecostalism was a shock to everyone.

In the eighties, my mother broke away from the Catholic Church at the urging of a close friend who convinced her she was following a false god. She found herself swept up in evangelical fervor, and when the tide took her, she pulled me along.

Our evangelical church had its roots in religious revivals that had transpired in the United States. Our pastors were white missionaries whose brand of fundamentalism favored the Old Testament.

My mother's fervor reached a fever pitch in the early nineties. Home became an open field upon which she rained fire and brimstone on the daily. Every week, she badgered my grandmother to remove her statue of the Virgin Mary from sight: *No dirty idols in my house*. Every week, Nana cried as she placed the statue back in the cupboard. We weren't allowed to showcase objects or paintings that portrayed faces: *The next to go will be that* Last Supper *painting of yours*.

The day James and Sharon, my mother's church friends, dropped by without prior notice, my grandmother was grieving the loss of her brother, who had died of unknown causes roughly a month prior. My mother told me he had been sent from doctor to doctor with excruciating headaches before passing away in a hospital bed.

James and Sharon told Nana that god had sent them. That they had come of their own accord—not sent by the church. That they had had a vision of her brother in a hospital bed, screaming in pain, cobras on either side of his head crushing his skull. They told her it was because he had married into a different religion and had therefore been cursed. They told her that god loved her and that he sent them to save her.

Nana, devastated and broken, believed them.

————•————

When you first see your grandma that day, she does not notice you.

She is sitting at the dining table. *The Last Supper*, which usually hangs above the head of the table at mealtime, lays flat in front of her. Broken glass is strewn across the dining table. The scene is a puzzle of elements you try to piece together.

It is then you notice that she is carrying a hammer, and you realize that she has smashed the painting. The symbol of her faith—in shards.

Give in to Christ, James says, hand on her shoulder. *You don't want to cling to idols.*

She bursts into a howl of tears that makes your hair stand and takes a second swing. It splinters glass across the room. The action is, in part, shocking because your grandmother has never been anything if not gentle all the time you've known her.

She puts the hammer down, looks up, and notices you. She wipes away her tears. She wears your mother's vacant smile.

———————•———————

It took me years to realize that perhaps the reason I love horror is the fact that when I was twelve years old, I was subjected to it.

The first time I watched *The Exorcist,* it never occurred to me that demon-filled Regan was the same age when she was exorcised. Like mine, her single mother did not know what else to do with her daughter's deviant behavior.

I love many things about the film—its questions concerning faith, caregiving, the limitations of science. What I enjoy less is watching a young girl's body used as a battleground for the wills of male authority figures: doctors declaring disease, demon defiling flesh, a pair of priests fighting for her soul in the name of a male-godhead. Through all this, Regan's mother waits and watches.

The further into the movie we get, the less her body is seen as her own, and the more fraught and violent her relationship with her mother becomes.

There is nothing like a horror film to reveal the cultural anxieties of one's time and place. And if horror has taught me anything, it is that nothing has been as enduringly terrifying across time and place as women's bodies, as the bodies of all marginalized genders.

I learned in church that when it comes to possession, women and children are the most vulnerable. Imagine the doubly devilish potential of a girl-child—this evil body, this heinous vessel, in need of emptying out.

————◆————

What they do not understand when they come to your house is that you have lived your whole life with ghosts. The father who leaves your mother, his body found hanging from a ceiling years later. Your half siblings, who are strangers living in a commune two countries away. Your mother, who decided that in order to be whole she had to lose herself to god, an invisible man who would be by her side after every other man had left.

No wonder they come to your house looking for ghosts. Ghosts are spilling out of the walls.

Once they are done with your grandma, they tell you to take a shower and put on some fresh clothes. You emerge from the bathroom in a shirt and bermuda shorts. You stand slouched, thumbs in your pockets. They look you up and down. In that moment, you know what they're here for.

They speak to your mother, gesturing at you, telling her things she already knows. How you speak *like a boy*, swagger *like a boy*. Fit yourself into *boy*-clothes to be one of the *boys*.

It's the demons, they say, gesticulating manically. *We need to get them out.*

You want to run, but where would you go? You are twelve years old and anywhere you might try to escape to will end with you back here.

You look at your mother, raise your voice over theirs: *Don't let them do anything to me.*

She ignores you.

———•———

Cinematic horror is laden with mothers trying to discipline their demonic daughters. Consider Carrie White, the titular character in the film *Carrie*, whose mother is convinced that her daughter's telekinetic powers are from the devil. She locks her in the closet and makes her pray for forgiveness. She projects onto Carrie her own shame—the humiliation of having had a child out of wedlock, of having her child's father leave them both in the lurch. She tells Carrie not to go to the prom. Warns her that no one could possibly love her. That she is being lured there by classmates who want to laugh at her expense.

She is not wrong. Carrie, after all, is the ultimate victim, bullied in school and abused at home. Wherever Carrie goes, she carries the consequences of her own body. In school she is "ugly," awkward, repulsive to her fellow students. At home, her flesh is a repository of sin, blossoming with evil, ripe for wickedness.

In the film's arguably most famous sequence, Carrie is crowned prom queen—a cruel plan to get her onstage—when a rigged bucket filled with pig's blood is emptied onto her in front of the whole school.

The crowd is stunned into silence, and then erupts into laughter. We see them from Carrie's point of view. Fragmented images of students and staff. Their unrepentant glee.

They're all gonna laugh at you!

No one's going to laugh at me, Mama.

Carrie stands onstage, hair dripping blood, satin dress drenched red. Her body revolts.

The gym doors slam shut. The harsh spray of a fire hose forces everyone to their knees. Pandemonium. She descends from the stage, eyes bulging with rage, arms stiff by her sides. Whatever she looks at, she controls. The mic short-circuits. The open electrical current catches flame.

The start of the fire is the beginning of the end. She is the only one to emerge from the gym. Behind her, flames lick its insides clean. The exterior walls of the school are decorated with huge silver stars. She looks like she is walking out from a nightmare and into a dream.

Mama was right. Carrie makes her way home. She wants her mama. She wants to cry. She wants to say sorry. She wants to be held.

Her mother waits for her at home, knife in hand.

———•———

When I turn thirty-six, my mother dies.

It is not a surprise. She has been dying for months and I've been getting texts and messages urging me to go see her.

Not counting my grandmother's funeral, I have not seen my mother in fifteen years. The texts come from church members I've not seen in twenty. I block every person who finds me on social media, save every phone number as "Don't Pick Up."

People tell me that death softens troubled relationships. This does not ring true with me. My resolve not to engage is fortified when I receive one of several messages coaxing me to the hospital with the promise of my mother wanting to make amends.

The message comes from one of the people who exorcised me. I decide not to go.

After my mother dies, I go back to her apartment to clear out her things. Amidst three decades' worth of accumulated life, I find a book about "how to bring your adult child back to Christ."

I have never really believed in god, but I do believe in the ability of religion to magnify within a person what already exists. Perhaps that in itself is a sort of supernatural occurrence, a sort of otherworldly power.

When I meet with a cousin to discuss legal matters, she tells me that because I was not there when my mother died, my mother took the liberty of "forgiving herself" for what she did to me. Given that she clearly had no change of heart in all the time I was gone, I have no idea what she forgave herself for.

———————•———————

When I think about troubled mother-daughter relationships, I often think about Robert Eggers's *The Witch*.

Seventeenth-century New England: a Puritan family departs from their church and village over differences of opinion regarding scripture. Sixteen-year-old Thomasin, her parents, and her three younger siblings find themselves living isolated on the edge of a forest—a danger zone full of the unknown.

We will conquer the wilderness, Thomasin's father says. *It will not consume us.*

Over the course of the film, Thomasin's siblings are picked off one by one by unknown forces that her mother attributes to witchcraft. The deeper into the film we go, the more convinced Thomasin's mother is that Thomasin is the witch.

She is half-right.

As viewers, we know from the very beginning that there are witches in the forest who have afflicted the family with curses, stolen the children, ground their bodies into salve. We know they dash through the dark of the woods, run rife with magic and mayhem. But most important, we know Thomasin is not one of them, even as her family members are killed off one by one and only Thomasin and her mother remain. Her mother, fully convinced now that Thomasin has sold her soul to the devil, pounces on her daughter, pushes her flat onto the ground, accusing her of killing her family. She hits her repeatedly across the face and tries to choke her. Thomasin does not know what has killed her family, so amidst the blows her mother inflicts, she yells desperately through tears the one thing she does know:

No, Mother, I love you.

Unable to fight off her mother's blows and desperate to live, she grabs the cleaver that lays on the ground and swings it into her mother's head. Thomasin weeps, sits in shock for the rest of the day, a girl by herself at the edge of a forest. A girl whose whole family is dead.

Hopeless, angry, and tired when evening falls, she calls out to the devil, the conspirator her mother seemed so desperate to align her with, daring him to speak. You think the film will end there, but it doesn't.

In the silence, a deep, droning voice emerges from the darkness: *What dost thou want?*

Thomasin, calm, responds softly: *What canst thou give?*

The voice asks if she would like to live deliciously.

She speaks one word: *Yes.*

In the film's final minutes, Thomasin strides naked, deeper and deeper into the woods. She comes upon a clearing. There, women writhe naked in pleasure around a blazing fire, chanting indecipherably. She joins them. They don't require an explanation and she does not offer one. She lets her body be consumed by the moment. Together in their circle, they chant, they laugh. And together, like the moon, they rise slowly into the sky.

The film's final shot is one of Thomasin's face. In her laughter, there is bliss, wonder. As the camera pulls away, we see her in the air. All around her, the tips of pine trees. Suspended, she stretches out her arms, inviting the wilderness into her chest. She is delirious with joy. She is free.

———————•———————

You don't yet know that you are on the brink of freedom. That your rage is what will get you there.

See how angry she is? they tell your mother. *That snarl is the devil.*

For some reason, this is what you remember most sharply from that day. Despite seven hours of being yelled at, of being manhandled. Of watching them burn your belongings on the kitchen stove. Of being told: *Your desire is the devil. Your clothes are the devil. Your body is the devil.* Despite this, years later, what will make your skin bristle with indignation is the memory of being told that even your rage is not your own, not your right, not a natural conclusion to this madness.

That snarl is the devil. It is at this moment that something inside you shifts. Confirms in your gut that all this is *wrong*. As a child, you have no language to parse this feeling, but you know in your body that it is true.

Like so many other things your body knows to be true but doesn't yet have words for. Like that feeling you had when you were nine and the pretty neighbor girl on the eighteenth floor smiled at you in the elevator. Or when you saw two women kissing on-screen for the first time when you were ten. Or when you went into your grandfather's closet when no one was home, and put on a pair of his trousers. They hung loose about you, looked ridiculous. But in them, you moved different, walked taller, sat wider, learned to take up space. You looked in the mirror, not knowing that your future would be full of these moments—moments in which something buried inside you would find its way to the surface, and smile back at you. That every single time, it would be like discovering treasure you didn't know you were looking for.

———————•———————

Seven hours into the exorcism, you understand that you are gay—a label that will eventually become too reductive to encompass everything you desire but for that moment is more than enough to fill your child-self. Before this day, all desire was a passing phase—something destined to fade with age. These people, what they think they have quelled, they have magnified. They've confronted you with your own reflection, explained you to yourself. And you understand that for this ordeal to end, you need to give in.

Do you understand that you are a sinner?

You speak one word: *Yes.*

What you keep to yourself is the fact that you don't care.

You are a sinner. And you don't care.

It is possibly the most adult thought you've had, and it is exhilarating—your first brush with feeling free. It transforms you. Intensifies your rage. Forces you unexpectedly into understanding. Between broken belongings and a broken heart, you learn quickly: when they say something inside you needs casting out, it is you they are referring to.

And that is fine. Because you will cast yourself from this place. You will conquer the wilderness and become it. You will revel in your rage, be consumed by the jaws of your own wild hunger. And it will be delicious. And there will be salvation yet.

One Size Fits Small

The nation needed us to be thin, and there was something
foreign about my body, something unpatriotic.
It was an early experience of queerness
and of abnormality.

—JOEL TAN, "FAT SHAME"

When I was eleven years old, Singapore implemented a weight loss program across all public schools, targeting "overweight" kids aged nine to sixteen. It was dubbed "The TAF Programme" by the country's Ministry of Education and was better known as "The TAF Club" in school. Pronounced "tough," TAF was an acronym for "Trim And Fit."

TAF.

Go ahead—spell that backwards!

The week students were streamed into TAF, we were summoned to the school clinic one by one to have our vital information recorded. Waists were measured and heights were taken. We were put on scales and pinched with vernier calipers. Checking against BMI charts, a school nurse decided whether or not we were overweight. According to her, I was "very fat," a piece of information I was already privy to. I'd heard it from the boys in my swimming class and at church; from my grandfather; from friends' parents; and most often, from my mother. Old news, even at that young age. Even then, I knew my fat body was fair game for commentary.

As a child, I understood that we were being put into this program to get us to lose weight. What I did not really comprehend at that age was the massive scale at which this program was being executed. An entire *nation* of public schools, to my knowledge largely unsupervised in how they enforced the program, were given fitness targets they were required to meet and, according to rumor, cash incentives if those requirements were exceeded. Across the country, fat kids and teens became problems that needed to be solved, and Singapore, pragmatic as usual, was out to solve them.

Different schools adopted their own approaches to the program, but for the most part, TAF was implemented daily as part of school life. Because of this, opting out was difficult and in some cases not possible. In some schools, kids with BMIs of 23 and above were forced into high-intensity exercise and food restriction during recess while the other kids ate. Some schools limited the food TAF kids were allowed to purchase from the school canteen. Other schools segregated TAF kids from their straight-size peers during recess so their eating could be monitored.

There was no single strategy employed across the board. However, the one component that seemed consistent across the board was shame.

———————◆———————

I sometimes forget how deeply fatphobic Singapore is. You would think that being part of a nationwide, government-initiated program like this would make forgetting hard, and that if this experience wasn't enough to jog my memory, I'd be reminded by everything else. Being turned down for a sales job without even an interview because the shop had no uniforms for my then size 12 body. Never finding affordable clothes as a teen because neighborhood stores and local brands seemed to always stop at size 10, often labeled XL. Strangers giving me health "advice" on the streets. Friends' parents "joking" about my body. Being summoned to the Ministry of Health every year as a primary school kid to be lectured about my weight. Never once seeing a fat person on local television in any context other than comedy. Remembering in particular the death of Rosnah, a peripheral character on *Under One Roof*,

Singapore's first locally produced English-language sitcom, which first aired in 1995—and how the writers explained her death in Season 6: choking while overeating at a buffet.

As a bonus, consider that all of this took place during a particularly cruel era of antifatness in American media and advertising—media largely consumed by English-speaking teens in Singapore at the time. The rise of supermodel Kate Moss paralleled the popularity of the "heroin chic" aesthetic, emaciated features and the hegemonic glorification of ultrathin bodies. "Fat Monica," despite her joyful and outgoing nature, was made a recurring joke in *Friends*—the undesirable, undesired, food-obsessed woman no one wanted to be, even when compared to her thin counterpart, who was characterized by neurosis and a petty sense of competition. Western "supermodel" culture trickled down into ours, and it seemed like every other company was looking for the "fresh new face" that would "change everything."

I remember a friend of mine entering the New Paper New Face competition when we were both seventeen years old—it was a model search organized by a local newspaper. I remember her crying as though her life were over when she got rejected. I remember feeling both devastated about and bewildered by her extreme reaction. She was thin and very attractive by conventional standards, and I could not understand how someone who looked like her could think herself ugly—a word she sobbed into the phone as we spoke.

I thought about that moment again, years later, while helping a local women's organization digitize their local media watch archives—which comprised extensive documentation of how women and women's bodies were represented in articles, interviews, and advertisements carried by the country's national newspapers. The sheer volume of advertising focused on everything deemed wrong with our bodies was astounding—an absolute verb salad insisting we tighten, lighten, shrink, straighten, whiten, tone, pluck, enhance, smooth, shave, laser off parts of ourselves for the greater good, for *our* greater good. A 2010 report I was asked to proofread noted not only a 30 to 50 percent increase in plastic surgery procedures done on people aged sixteen to twenty-five but also the fact that in 2007, the International Narcotics Control Board had found Singapore fifth on a list of countries with the highest per capita consumption of diet drugs. That same year, a *Singapore Medical Journal* survey of women and girls aged seventeen to twenty-two found that less than a quarter of respondents thought of themselves as being "the right weight."

But what was the "right weight"? Was it designated by BMI, a test that, for the most part, had been developed with reference to white bodies and has since been proven questionable as a measure of overall health? Was it lower than that, some unachievable number that would put us in league with the Kate Mosses of the world? Or were we just expected to shrink ourselves down to whatever size made us pass effortlessly through the world, unimposing, compliant, eager to please?

———◆———

I've never been the "right weight"—a fat kid right from when I was four years old. I started in the TAF Club my final two years of primary school and remained all through secondary school. In my school, TAF was conducted differently every year. One year, we were made to exercise during recess while others had their meals. Sometimes, these exercise sessions took place in the school hall. But many times, they were conducted on the concourse—the open area at the school's main drop-off point. The space was partially visible from the canteen, where all the other girls ate, right in front of the school carpark and the entrance to the primary school.

I never went. I figured that there were too many of us for any sort of legitimate attendance taking to be done during our brief recess breaks. Some girls shared about how embarrassing it was. But I did not skip sessions out of embarrassment. I skipped because going meant spending less time with the friends whose support was mitigating the trauma of my home life and the trauma of being my mother's daughter.

My mother probably had the greatest influence on my attitudes about beauty and body image. When I was nine, she started consuming diet drugs that she called "fat burners"—large brown pills that supposedly burned fat if you ate them before meals. Decidedly embarrassed by my size, she made me eat them too. She also purchased products such as the Abdominizer off Sell-a-Vision in a bid to lose weight and, when slimming treatments became a thing, subscribed to those as well. Anger was my default emotion as a teen and tween, and because being told what to do with my body and my time made me angry, my mother's obsession with body and beauty had an effect opposite to what she had intended. Everything in which she staunchly believed—thinness, heterosexuality, god—I wholeheartedly rejected.

My teen rebellion against everything she tried to impress upon me lasted well into my young adulthood. I suspect it was one of the reasons I started working as a life drawing model when I was nineteen. Yes, it paid better and faster than most of the part-time work I was doing as a student, but I also know that deep down inside, I was thrilled at the idea that my mother might find out I was getting naked for strangers—smug at the thought of offending every puritanical middle-class bone in her body. After all, she'd been the one to storm out of my room while I was writing a school paper about artist Lucian Freud, having spotted a printout of the painted nude I was analyzing in my essay.

"Get that filth out of my house."

The words dripped with disgust. Imagine how she would have reacted had it been my own fat body in that painting.

When I started life modeling, I had no idea how much I would enjoy it or that it would turn into a consistent source of income over the next ten years. I did it purely for the money and was surprised to learn that it was something I was actually good at. I'd studied life drawing for two semesters in school, so I had a rough idea of what artists wanted from models in order to make dynamic drawings. I learned that my body was flexible, that I had strong arms and strong legs, and that I could stay still for fairly long periods of time. Plus, for the first time in my life, my size was an asset. Art colleges and artists liked having a variety of models with different body types in rotation, and because fat models were hard to come by, I was always in rotation.

I thought a lot about my body while I was doing this work, especially at the beginning. How poses which appear so effortless can hurt like hell when sustained for more than ten minutes. How you can shift your weight imperceptibly from one side to the other while sustaining a standing pose. How, when I took off my clothes and took up space, my body was not a source of disgust but a puzzle to be worked out, skillfully, creatively, joyfully, on paper.

How this same body that my mother had wanted to shrink, and that the state had wanted to discipline, was keeping me alive and fed.

———————•———————

When I say I sometimes forget how deeply fatphobic Singapore is, I'm not being completely honest. What I really mean is that being immersed in that environment required me to normalize it in order to survive it. It remains shocking to me that I'm unable to locate an indepth study of how the TAF Programme may have harmed children and teenagers, or very much creative output addressing the trauma it may have caused individuals who were roped into it. At a time where everything is online, the sparse amount of content I encountered when I started my research made me doubt my own memories. If no one was talking about it, maybe I was making a bigger deal of it in my head than it actually was.

I log on to Twitter and relay some of my own TAF Club experiences, asking if anyone else remembers them. The responses come so fast and furious it triggers a panic attack, and I end up muting the thread shortly after, privatizing my account before the devil's advocates and concern trolls arrive. A journalist from the BBC picks up on the heat and contacts me for an interview. They want to write a piece about the impact of the TAF's approach on children while weaving in my experience as one of the leading voices. I decline almost immediately, realizing that I am not as brave as I had thought I was when I made the initial post. I don't want to open myself to any more scrutiny than the tweet has already garnered, and I wonder whether this is the reason that so few people have called the program out online. Maybe no one wants that scrutiny.

I scroll through reply after reply, retweet after retweet. As expected, because each school had their own approach to the program, reactions vary. However, while some people's experiences are neutral, their teachers having taken a very soft hand, most people's experiences are awful, and amidst the wave of replies, I see words like "torture," "ostracised," "self-hatred," and "bully."

One person recalls being made to show up early to school to walk up and down the stairs—their mother encouraged them to do this because they were immigrants and needed to "stay in line" as much as possible. One woman—a former student who won awards at the national level and played sports six days a week—was put in the program, called "fat," and told to eat less because her BMI was higher than normal. She would learn later in life that she had higher-than-normal bone density and muscle mass, and that having any less fat while she was a teen would have meant having too little. Another tweeter was not allowed to eat during recess—that was designated exercise time for those in the program. Another was allowed to sit only with other TAF students during recess while they all shared a box of cherry tomatoes.

Numerous people talked about how TAF precipitated body image issues; others mentioned how it put them off physical activity instead. One person explained how it accelerated an eating disorder, and another shared that in order to leave TAF, they had to lose 11 pounds *more than* the weight deemed "acceptable" by the program.

For some who were not part of the club, just the possibility of being forced into it was enough to inject the fear of fat into their hearts. One woman became hyperaware of her body when she was seven. Another remembers being fourteen and researching how she could get medically approved for liposuction.

I close Twitter angry that night. On the one hand, I want to hold space for everyone's stories. To listen and not judge. On the other, I want to know who the adults in these children's lives were. Who was there providing the support and counter-messaging they needed to hear?

I used to think that my mother in all her body shame was unique. But maybe she really was every parent.

Maybe that was the problem.

———•———

In my personal opinion, Singapore's habit of micromanaging the bodies of its citizens has been long-standing, not one relegated solely to TAF.

In his 1986 National Day Rally speech—an annual tradition not unlike the U.S.'s State of the Union address—Lee Kuan Yew, then prime minister, said:

"I am often accused of interfering in the private lives of citizens. Yes, if I did not, had I not done that, we wouldn't be here today. And I say without the slightest remorse, that we wouldn't be here, we would not have made economic progress, if we had not intervened on very personal matters—who your neighbour is, how you live, the noise you make, how you spit, or what language you use. We decide what is right."

And boy, was he not kidding about his love of intervention.

In the early seventies, the crude birth rate in Singapore rose from 22.1 to 23.1 births per 1,000 residents—this led to the two-child policy, which strongly encouraged couples not to have more than two children. On the heels of the campaign came the Voluntary Sterilisation Act, with the state introducing measures to increase the number of people willing to undergo sterilization. Among its measures, priority in primary school registration for their children was given to sterilized parents. The Employment Act was also amended to ensure that women with two or more living children were no longer eligible for paid maternity leave. In addition to this, under the Sterilisation Act, people living with certain hereditary illnesses could be sterilized without consent at the request of a parent or spouse, so long as a doctor certified that the sterilization was necessary in the interest of the person and society.

Conversely, in the eighties, the state became concerned that "better-educated" women were not having *enough* children and were remaining single. As a response, it established the Social Development Unit—a dating network dedicated to matching unmarried university graduates working in public service. In addition, under the Graduate Mothers' Priority Scheme, kids of university-educated mothers with at least three children would receive top priority in primary school registration. Slightly later, a parallel scheme known as the Small Family Incentive Scheme aimed to encourage parents without any O-level passes to get sterilized. Women under thirty who agreed to undergo sterilization could apply for a $10,000 incentive.

Up until today, the hand of the Singaporean government reaches even into one's home. Walking around naked in your own apartment with the curtains open is a criminal act, subject to imprisonment should someone who sees you from the outside choose to report you. The same hand that makes its way into your home extends beyond the country's borders. Testing positive for drug consumption means imprisonment even if consumption occurred outside of Singapore, in a country where it was legal.

It often feels like overreach of authority is part of who we are as a country—fingerprints of the state on our skin are an everyday reality internalized and normalized. No one spoke up about the TAF Club because it was not an aberration but a norm. If your body is not acting the way it is supposed to, what other option is there but for the government to intervene?

One's body may be a personal matter. But the government decides what is right.

To be honest, at thirteen, being fat was not a problem I considered high on my radar of things to be concerned about. Because apart from the rules dictated by TAF, our convent school had a few of its own, many of which were developed the year "all-girl" secondary schools ended up featured on the front pages of the national tabloids with a photo of two girls wearing our uniforms, holding hands at a bus stop, their faces blurred.

The headline read: "Do All-Girl Secondary Schools Encourage Lesbianism?"

What came next was what some of my schoolmates and I referred to as the "Lesbian Elimination Squad."

LES.

You don't even need to spell it backwards!

LES referred to the actions the school was taking in reaction to the article—actions we learned about during Monday morning assembly. Our school counselor ranted about the headlines into a microphone, and we were told that anyone found to be in a relationship with another girl would be forced to break up, and would be sent straight to counseling. Worse, her parents would be informed. In addition to a ban on same-sex relationships, girls were not allowed to have hair that was "too short," to sport undercuts, or to be found wearing a chest binder.

I was mortified. I knew I liked girls but hadn't told anyone yet. I felt alone and exposed, listening to the anger and disgust with which the counselor spoke. But that was when I heard something that has stayed with me ever since that moment. From the other side of the hall, murmurs arose from a handful of older girls. They grew in volume and were distinct in tone.

Oh my god. Were they . . . *heckling*? They *were* heckling! Boos and laughter.

The counselor went red in the face. I don't know who the hecklers were. And the teachers were unable to identify them among the sea of students. But I remember how hearing them made me feel. It was as if I'd been holding my breath, too scared to breathe—and then someone laughed, and I was able to exhale.

To this day, I think of that moment as formative—it taught me how important it is to speak up whenever possible. That you never know who you are helping when you voice dissent, that you never know who is listening. Being queer and fat were separate issues, but both TAF and LES taught me the same lesson: that my body was state property, that it needed to be punished and trained into compliance. Those heckling girls taught me that not everyone agreed, that I did not have to comply.

———◆———

The memory of that small resistance was still with me a year later when another member of staff took to the microphone.

It was my PE teacher. This was the same woman who had recently singled out the fat girls in class to let us know in front of our classmates that losing weight was not only about health but also about intelligence: we would soon be streamed into either arts or science classes, and, according to her, overweight students were generally less smart and always ended up in the arts. According to her, not only was being fat a failure but going into the arts was a failure as well.

I learned during that assembly that, contrary to my assumptions about PE instructors, this one *had* been taking attendance at TAF Club after all, and that she was holding a list of names of the girls who had not been attending class all semester. She called our names out one by one, telling us to stand up. As each of us rose she read our respective weights into the mic in front of our whole school. She also mentioned how much we were *supposed* to weigh in contrast, and mathematically how "overweight" we were in percentage terms. She informed us that she was adding in those details to highlight how much we needed to attend TAF sessions.

I think that if I had not heard those girls heckling the year before, this moment might have devastated me. Instead, I got angry, not just for myself, but for all the girls who were made to stand up. I noticed a classmate of mine, also standing, who had tears in her eyes and was trying to cover her face. I whisper-called her as the PE teacher continued on her rampage.

"Hey," I said, trying to look reassuring, trying to focus on what I understand now to be solidarity. "Fuck them."

She met my gaze and I mimed the teacher's grouchy face. My classmate laughed a little through her tears, and I think we both felt better.

———•———

Supportive community is important in any situation where different means damaged. I know because skipping TAF sessions was often a community effort. In the canteen, I sat with the same seven or eight friends every day and the routine was always the same—we tucked into our food, trying to finish as fast as possible amidst conversation and laughter. Recess was thirty-five minutes and in that time, you'd have to queue to purchase your food, consume it, return your plates, and line up in pairs on the school field before filing back to class row by row. And sometimes, during recess, our PE teacher, somehow omnipotent, would find time away from TAF even though she was running it, to come to the canteen to hunt for the girls who were absent. How this would usually go down was that one of my friends would spot her, let me know in a panic, and I would duck, slide myself off the bench, go hide in a corner, plate still in hand, mouth still chewing, and reemerge only once she was gone.

My friends were all thin, all conventionally attractive, but they never made me feel bad about my body or myself. The matter never came up during meals, or when we changed for PE, or when I could not find clothes in my size. I don't think any of us really had the language for what was inherently wrong with TAF Club. Terms like "fat-shaming" or "fatphobia" weren't really a thing yet, and we hadn't had any conversations explicitly about bodily autonomy or body image, but there seemed to be an implicit understanding of the fact that if a teacher was forcing you to do something that did not involve studying, it was not cool and it was important to have each other's backs.

In short, we were allies. And still today, when I seek out friendship, what I am really seeking are allies. To be a friend is to be a conspirator. As friends, we were accountable to one another.

———◆———

A lot of people think of the TAF Programme as having been a success. After all, by 2002, a decade into its existence, it had reduced the obesity rate of students in Singapore by 4.2 percent. And if that was the measure of success for which it was created, who am I to argue?

To my knowledge, there is no documentation of whether students who lost weight over the course of the program kept it off once they passed through the education system. Nor could I find information about the students who were part of the program but who did not reach their ideal weights. Had they lost weight, but not enough? Had the program had an opposite effect on them?

Surprisingly, with the exception of one study, there has not been much research into the program's contribution to eating disorders, body image issues, or the stigma of growing up fat in a country where one size fits small—at least not that I have found. The most readily available study that mentions TAF is an eight-year retrospective of anorexia nervosa in Singapore which found that instances of anorexia nervosa and bulimia increased sixfold between 1994 and 2002 and that 11.1 percent of the subjects seen for these disorders were former members of the TAF Club. In addition, Wikipedia, as trustworthy as it may or may not be, will tell you that a week following the release of this study, a National University of Singapore study of 4,400 schoolgirls revealed a direct link between the TAF Club and disordered eating—however no sources for this statement remain available online. The same Wikipedia entry mentions that the Ministry of Education was quick to deny these findings.

TAF was discontinued in 2007, ten years after I left secondary school. Looking back, I am struck most strongly by how young we were when we were put through it. We were kids singled out by adults, bullied and shamed in front of peers, made to feel like we were less-than, made targets by the very people who were supposed to be educating us.

Fear of being scrutinized—not just for being fat, but for calling out a government program as having been harmful—still fills my belly as I write the essay. But I want to be accountable to my child-self, even though I came out pretty unscathed compared to many peers who clearly weren't as lucky.

For the TAF kids who never recovered from the instilled shame of being fat, who lived or live through disordered eating, who experience body dysmorphia, who look into the mirror and still see someone who is not enough because they were once deemed too much, I ask:

Who is accountable to them?

I Had a Dream I Was Your Hero

I was twelve years old the first time I heard a woman sing a love song to another woman. It was Sophie B. Hawkins performing "Damn, I Wish I Was Your Lover," and it was the final line of the first verse that hooked me:

I had a dream I was your hero.

Like many kids, I had been told fairy tales that involved heroes—namely, princes rescuing princesses from villains. And ironically, it was within these archaic parameters that I perhaps first experienced queerness. In all my fairy-tale–informed daydreams, I was always the hero. And I was always rescuing whoever my best friend was at the time from some sort of bad situation. When I was a younger kid, she needed saving from either an evil teacher or the creepy man that allegedly lurked at the borders of our convent school gate. In my tweens, the narratives got more complex and she usually needed saving from a bad household or a bully.

As a child, I hadn't yet begun to think about fairy tales as prescriptions for gender roles or patriarchal narratives—all I knew was that I had no interest in being saved by a prince. And so in this heteronormative world of children's stories in which I had no place, I had somehow managed to carve out a role for myself, queering the gender binary in my own small way while falling into an equally false one: that of hero and victim.

It took me a while to learn that if I wasn't a girl that needed saving, other girls probably weren't either.

And if that was the case, what role was I supposed to play?

Truth be told, "Damn, I Wish I Was Your Lover" was not the first song I heard in which a woman sang to another woman. It was just the first song in which I picked up on that dynamic.

The *real* first time was when I was eleven. I was at a birthday party, and the birthday girl made us all play a sordid board game called Girl Talk. The board was colored flu-pill pink, and the game involved taking turns to spin a wheel, pick up a card, and perform a task.

Turn on the radio. The song that is playing will be the song that will play when you fall in love.

That's the first card I got. And the song was "Constant Craving" by k.d. lang. I had heard it before but didn't know the title or have any idea who the singer was. I had certainly not seen the black-and-white video that spliced reenactments from Samuel Beckett's *Waiting for Godot* with scenes of lang, handsome and brooding, crooning about the perpetuity of her hunger.

At thirteen I saw the video for the first time and listened properly to the lyrics. I was embarrassed by the track's unabashed longing—the idea that desire could be this dark and constant a thing, "marching brave," beneath one's skin. Lang's pained expressions, her sorrowful off-camera gaze, her running of fingers through her hair—they embarrassed me too. She was so beautiful and so striking—a combination of short hair, soft fabric, and sharp lines.

I had never seen anyone like her. All the butch girls in my school who wore surf tees and basketball shorts, rat-tails and wallet chains, who were rowdy and swaggering—I loved them, but they were teenagers. Young enough so that adults around us could wave them off as "tomboys" and further perpetuate the idea that everything queer was a teenage phase.

But lang was a grown-ass adult. She was successful and on TV. And if there was something in her desire that was more than just a phase, then maybe there was something in mine that would live into the future.

———•———

By seventeen I am one of those queers who has come out with a vengeance. I am angry and frustrated and a junior college dropout. I am also obsessed with Melissa Etheridge.

I discover her at a CD shop in Centrepoint. I've heard her name and I've heard she's gay, but I've never really listened to her music. It's interesting that the shop does not have any of her more famous albums—what they do have is a live album recorded in 1995 that looks and sounds suspiciously like it was bootlegged. It becomes the only thing I have in my Discman for a month.

On many tracks, her voice is hot with jealousy and rage, love and desire. The recording captures the energy of the audience, and hearing women scream for this woman singing about women is unexpectedly sexy and even more unexpectedly liberating.

I save up money and buy all her albums, and I love every single one of them. It's weird how much resonance there seems to be between her experience of growing up gay in small-town America and my experience of growing up gay on this tropical city-island. I listen to her song "Nowhere to Go"—the line "this hell is not mine" becomes a mantra. It's the first time I have loved a musician this much since Alanis Morissette raged her way into my life. Alanis makes me want to write poetry. Melissa makes me want to be the gayest version of myself.

So when I get into art school—my first experience of school without a uniform—I do the most cliché thing one can do. I shave off all my hair, making my mother cry. She's already dealt with the boots and the torn jeans and rainbow-laden bag, but this is one step too far. I notice immediately how differently I pass through the world. A bald head, a hairstyle reserved for eighteen-year-old boys doing compulsory military service, is an affront to people when it's mine. Men queuing behind me for the public phone make jokes and call me an "it." Women do double takes when I walk into public toilets. Male classmates make sarcastic remarks.

You would think that in art school, people who look "different" are less of an anomaly. But in Singapore, for the most part, it's business as usual. My head becomes a filter that helps eliminate me from small talk with conservative classmates since no one wants to speak to the weirdo-slash-lesbian. What I thought was an expression of queerness becomes indicative not just of sexual desire but also of all the ways I inconvenience the well-oiled machine of polite society. In my teenage angst, I could not be happier about this.

I remind myself that this hell is not mine.

———————◆———————

To this day, the Singapore media machine remains tightly controlled, and positive representations of queer characters remain prohibited on public television. Broadcasting a show that includes a "same-sex" kiss or a happy and hopeful same-sex family can result, and has resulted, in fines of up to $15,000. Last time I checked, the Media Development Authority's reasons for its restrictions were "community guidelines" developed through surveys—in my humble opinion, a way of shifting blame to the public. For years, the country's ruling party used similar reasoning for the retention of Section 377a, which criminalized sex between men: the idea that society was not ready.

Are queer people not part of society?

Film theorist Andrew Scahill says that queer spectators learn to be scavengers. I believe that this is true and that we learn to scavenge early on. We read queerness into characters who are outcasts, who dress differently, who are bullied. We read queerness into that which is desperate, liminal—into monsters and ghosts if we have to. I spent adolescence hungry and aching, craving some mirror-morsel of myself. We all did, not just across film, but also across the landscapes of our everyday lives.

At thirteen I had not heard of hanky codes or femme flagging, but if a girl had a single earring on her left lobe, I took a second look. If she wore a plaid shirt or basketball jersey, I took a second look. There was my mom's friend with the mullet and swagger. My cousin with the motorcycle who left for Europe and never returned. The woman who ran the bookshop in my primary school—her smart trousers and batik shirts.

But the special thing about queer people is that even though we scavenge for crumbs, we're also the ones who leave them in our wake. A glance. A button. A cheeky reference. A subtle lyric. You can try to make us disappear, but we find ourselves in one another again, and again, and again.

———•———

When George Michael dies in 2016, Cyril Wong, Singapore's first openly queer confessional poet, posts a public Facebook note commemorating his love for the gay icon. He writes about encountering Michael for the first time through VHS recordings of MTV, about growing up queer in Singapore, and about ideas of belonging. Through the piece, he weaves in the lyrics of "Father Figure," a song he encountered as a boy and instinctively knew was queer.

He notes that the chorus manages to be erotic, tender, urgent, hungry, and generous at the same time. Michael offers himself as preacher and teacher. And just like how Sophie B. Hawkins casts herself as both "mother" and "lover," Michael offers the gift of a father figure to his would-be lover.

Queer people have always found family in one another. Because our first experiences of family are often challenging at best and violent at worst, we become each other's parents, siblings, children. We relearn love from one another. We relearn belonging from one another. We learn that family is chosen and that blood runs thin. We choose each other over and over.

Like Michael, Hawkins is interchangeably seductive, nurturing, generous, and vulnerable in her relationship to the woman she sings to. She wants to save her from an abusive relationship and ease her pain. She wants to rock her till the daylight comes. She describes herself as too shy, too young, a schoolboy as she stands on a street corner waiting for her luck to change.

Michael offers: "Whatever you ask for, that's what I'll be."

Hawkins echoes: "I am everything."

———•———

I still remember the first time I listened carefully to "Damn, I Wish I Was Your Lover" and that moment in which everything I suspected about the song was confirmed. I was sitting at my desk and the song, scratchy and soft, was playing on my small red radio-cassette player.

She sang about making love to someone. She used the word "her."

I dropped my pencil and just stared at the radio.

I was twelve years old. There was no internet with which to search out lyrics. And even listening to the radio at home was already a risk with a mother who forbade secular music. The moment was there. And then it was gone.

Had the censors missed it? Or had I misheard it? Did a woman just sing about having sex with another woman on the radio?

Hawkins was certainly my hero that day because I felt saved by that song. The same way I have felt saved by every other bread crumb of queer confession I've scavenged since then.

At the end of his note about George Michael, Wong offers a tender invitation to other queers: "You can be my daddy, or I can be yours."

I offer something similar: I can be your hero, and you can be mine.

Because fuck leaving bread crumbs.

I want to leave a feast.

I Hope We Shine On

The email comes unexpected. Two and a half years following my mother's death. When I first describe the experience of receiving it, I say it comes as a shock to the system, but that is not exactly true. The feeling is more akin to disorientation, except that I'm not the one that has been displaced. It feels like looking down at your lap and finding a package you did not expect to see there. Something that is not yours but is addressed to you nonetheless.

The email is from my half sister, whom I've never met. I recognize her name immediately. It's a name I've googled on and off for years along with two others that belong to half brothers I have also never met.

The word "sister" sounds like an abstract impossibility to someone who spent her whole life being an only child. So instead of calling her "sister," let's agree on a pseudonym. Let's call her "Sky."

Sky has read an essay I wrote about my mother's death in an online journal. In it, I mention our shared father, his death by suicide. She tells me that her (our) older brother (let's call him "Joshua") recently died by suicide as well, having jumped from an apartment building. She tells me about her own experience with depression, that she sees her feelings in my writing, that her mother passed around the same time as mine. She tells me that her (our) brother who jumped was like me—a writer.

She says she's always thought it would be nice to have a sister. She tells me that she hopes I am happy.

The email seems to desire response, which sends me into fight or flight. I settle on flight, my version of which is a slow drift into feeling nothing. The numbness allows me to function, to do what I feel needs to be done, which in this case is to leave the email unanswered.

Prior to the email, the idea that I might one day meet my three half siblings has always lingered as an amorphous possibility in the back of my mind. But now, one of them is gone forever, and just like how I will never meet my father, I will never meet him. What was once an open ending is now a closed book.

No matter how hard I try not to, I keep thinking about the last line of her email.

I hope you are happy.

———————•———————

I don't know if I am happy. But one thing I am certain of when I close that email is that I am a terrible person. Because the first thing I do after is suss out Sky's Facebook page in order to do the calculations.

How old was Joshua when he died? Was he the same age as my father?

Turns out he was.

Some survival mechanism inside of me churns out selfish and illogical reassurance. I am past the age at which both father and brother killed themselves. In my mind, this mathematics is a sort of irrational pseudoscience that assures me I am out of the woods—surely if I have not killed myself by now, I never will. I relay this thought process to a friend, who points out that I am talking about their deaths as though they are results of some sort of curse. Ironic, since that is exactly how my mother, whom I try my best not to be anything like, viewed all chronic and mental illnesses—as curses we bring upon ourselves.

Most people familiar with my work know two formative things about my life: that my mother tried to have the gay exorcised out of me when I was a kid and that my father died by suicide when I was nine years old. What most people don't know is what my family told me: that nine years before he died, he left my mother for another woman and subsequently joined a cult. When he hanged himself, he left behind a second wife and three more children. As an adult, I learn the cult had communes all over the world, eventually became notorious for its systemic sexual abuse of children and more recently, like many other cults, the high suicide and addiction rates of those who manage to leave. Like many cults that came out of North America in the sixties and seventies, it started as an alternative, peace-loving, hippie-adjacent version of Christianity before it morphed into what was, for some members, a living nightmare.

What are the chances of being born to two parents whose separate paths would eventually lead them to different forms of religious extremes? You'd think two people so ironically similar would stay together.

I never met my father. But his death was a dark cloud hanging over my own suicidal ideation whenever I put blade to skin. Always at the tail end of so many unasked questions: Why am I like this? Why am I doing this? Why can't I stop?

When people ask me when I started self-harming, I tell them I was sixteen. *Were you sad?* they often ask. The first time the question is posed, I surprise myself with my answer. *No,* I tell them. *I was in love.*

It's true. I was so deeply in love. And she loved me back. I was so happy— my first real taste of pure elation—that all I could think of in my moments without her was what would happen if she left me.

When I cleared out my mother's apartment following her death, I saw something I had not seen in fifteen years and had completely forgotten about—the center of the linoleum floor of my bedroom violently shredded up. I had done that with a knife in my tweens because I was so full of anger and it was the only thing I knew how to do. I only stopped cutting up the floor when I started turning the knife on myself.

It was that memory that induced yet another memory. One that made me realize I'd been giving people wrong answers. I was actually twelve going on thirteen the first time I self-harmed. My primary school friends and I had moved to secondary school together, and I loved them the way many young teenagers love things—with do-or-die intensity. All my feelings bordered on obsession. My love included recurring and pervasive thoughts about one of my friends dying or moving away or getting sick, and these thoughts would make me cry myself to sleep at night. One day I took a penknife and carved the name of our little clique into my forearm. I did it lightly, afraid to leave a lasting mark.

The self-harm continued from my teens into my adulthood, and at some point in my twenties, after several years of struggling for money, moving from house to house, and dealing with declining mental health, I was pretty sure being dead was easier than being alive. I fantasized about death often. Everything was a chore and the physical pain of cutting made the emotional pain of being alive easier. Even though the immediate relief was followed the next day by deep regret.

I was twenty-seven the day I realized how severely depressed I was. I had slashed myself across the thigh so deeply and so many times, I killed two rags cleaning up the blood on the floor. A close friend, knowing I was having a hard month but unaware that this was happening, showed up unannounced at my door with soup. I could not bring myself to open the door, and turned her away.

I wanted change but I did not know how to get it. I wasn't able to afford a therapist and, more important, I did not want any government record of me being mentally ill because I did not trust that records would be confidential and that they would not affect any government teaching jobs I might have to apply for if I was out of work. Worse, I did not want to end up with some therapist giving me the number of some religious "help" group.

I was forty and in Canada the first time I spoke to a doctor about mental illness. Living through the ongoing Covid-19 pandemic had started to make every day feel like the verge of a breakdown. I gave detailed accounts of my history of self-harm, and she told me that based on the early onset of symptoms, as well as my father's suicide, the depression I lived with was likely hereditary.

All this time, I thought my father had left me with nothing, not even a memory with his face in it.

And yet, all this time, he'd left me something so deeply a part of me, it took me forty years to find.

———•———

In 2019, almost forty years after Stanley Kubrick releases his adaptation of Stephen King's *The Shining*, Mike Flanagan releases his own adaptation of King's sequel, *Doctor Sleep*.

Doctor Sleep reacquaints readers and viewers with Danny Torrance, the young boy in *The Shining*, who has survived both the supernatural violence of the Overlook Hotel and the parental violence of his father, Jack Torrance. Now middle-aged, with both of his parents dead, Danny continues to possess a psychic ability known as the Shining. He lives with alcohol addiction, like his father once did, and continues to be haunted by the ghosts of the Overlook. He also becomes acquainted with a young girl named Abra, who possesses the same psychic abilities he does, and the True Knot, a group of once-humans who live for centuries by feasting on the energies of children who shine. Literal psychic vampires, if you like.

In short, adult Danny is forced to make a decision: Does he choose to help Abra battle the True Knot, in turn risking his own life? Or does he choose to walk away? What happens when doing the right thing means having to return to the places of one's own trauma—in Danny's case, the Overlook Hotel?

While I love the chilling terror and artistry of Kubrick's *Shining*, it is a completely different sort of story from King's original novel—a tragic tale about addiction, family, loss, and intergenerational trauma that manages to function as both a terrifying horror story and a familial tragedy. And what I love about Flanagan's adaptation of the sequel is that in its final half hour, it uses the visual vocabulary of Kubrick's film to bring the story back to the spirit of King's original novel, essentially uniting them. He does this by re-creating sets and scenes from Kubrick's *Shining*, and making present-day *Doctor Sleep* characters occupy them in ways that embed these old spaces with new meanings.

With these "reoccupations," Flanagan creates an effective visual metaphor for trauma reenactment—an expression of unresolved trauma some people develop in which they reenact aspects of a traumatic incident in order to overcome it. In these scenes, Danny finds himself having to battle the literal and metaphorical ghosts of his childhood as a middle-aged man, in the same spaces that his parents experienced violence in *The Shining*. In these scenes of reenacted violence, he alternates between the roles of aggressor and victim.

The seeds of this running motif—reenactment—are planted early on in the film, with Danny being interviewed for a job in an office that is almost identical to the one his father was interviewed in when seeking work from the Overlook Hotel. While the original scene takes place in the seventies, the new scene takes place in the present day, making the stylings of the room feel aptly trapped in time, a ghostly apparition of something that came before, and a suggestion of history possibly repeating itself.

But the scene in which Flanagan fully leans into notions of history repeating itself takes place in the hotel's Gold Room. There, Danny, sober, visits the same hotel bar his father once did in *The Shining* and encounters his father's ghost in the form a bartender. The scene is incredibly painful to watch. Jack, who no longer remembers Danny, offers his sober son a drink the same way Lloyd, the bartender from

The Shining, once offered sober Jack a drink so many years before—the drink that eventually led to his downfall.

Danny resists. In response, Jack tells Danny that alcohol is *medicine*, a term that alludes to drink as a coping mechanism but also a euphemism used in *The Shining* to refer to the violence Jack showers upon his "disobedient" family. He goes on, saying that a wife and son are *so many mouths to feed* and that *these mouths eat time, eat away at your life,* are *enough to make you sick.* Danny's adult face as he holds back tears is so full of hurt that in it we also see the face of the scared and abused child he once was. For me, this scene is the film's beating heart, and what follows—the final confrontation sequence—is the blood that pumps through its veins.

Following the scene at the bar, Danny goes on to battle Rose, the leader of the True Knot. The battle almost entirely comprises reoccupations in which his experiences alternate in mirroring those of his father and those of his mother:

The Shining	*Doctor Sleep*
Jack Torrance stalks his wife up the main stairs of the hotel, threatening violence as she tries to defend herself with a bat.	Rose stalks Danny Torrance up the main stairs of the hotel, threatening violence as he tries to defend himself with an ax.

The Shining	*Doctor Sleep*
Jack's wife swings the bat. Jack falls down the stairs. She runs away. He picks himself up, extra enraged, and proceeds to go on a violent rampage, trying to search out and kill both her and Danny.	Danny swings the ax. Rose grabs it from him and swings. Hit, Danny falls down the stairs. He conquers her using the ghosts of the hotel, who in turn possess him. He proceeds to go on a violent rampage, stalking and trying to kill Abra.

It is hard to describe how harrowing the scenes of Danny stalking Abra are. How he limps through the corridor of the hotel, an injured predator wielding an ax, embodying exactly his father's monstrosity. How deeply he wants to inflict this same violence on a child the way his father once did upon him.

The entire sequence is imbued with a sense of hopelessness and dread. For me, it is also infused with questions of inevitability. Are we all destined to become our parents? Do they persist in their unfinished business from beyond the grave? Is to live in resistance of my genetic inheritance still to live haunted by it?

When do I become my own person?

———————◆———————

Long before I am contacted by Sky, long before my self-harming habit reaches its peak in my late twenties, long before I start thinking about trauma, depression, and genetic inheritance, I connect with the ghost of my father in an unexpected way.

I am an art school undergrad and I've started working with photocopy transfers—a type of printmaking that enables one to transfer photographic images to wood or paper using thinner. You make a photocopy of an image you want to print, place the copy facedown on the surface you are transferring it to, and sponge thinner onto the back of the image. When you lift the photocopy, you are left with a mirror image of the original—not perfect or exact in detail, but unmistakable in terms of its source.

The process has a sense of immediacy to it that is extremely satisfying. I end up making books and books of transferred images flanked by poetry. They end up kind of clichéd—the images stiflingly pretty, the poetry horribly overwrought. The combination is almost offensively decorative. The most cringeworthy thing about it is perhaps the fact that the project revolves around a woman I've fallen in love with and have spent the past month photographing.

One afternoon, during this same period of time, I find myself scavenging my mother's desk for my birth certificate in anticipation of my eventual departure from home. I don't find it. What I discover instead is a smooth square of cut, varnished wood. Beneath layers of gloss is a photocopy transfer of an image of my mother. It is flanked by poetry in almost the exact same format as the pages of the book I am making. My father's signature is at the bottom. The piece is dated 1979.

It is odd seeing something of myself locked in an object created before I was born. And while I understand that coincidence does not signify correlation, it makes me wonder what sorts of explanations about who I am are floating in my body. Was my father depressed when he killed himself? Was there language for this during his day? Is his depression mine? Is he the reason I've thought of death so many times over the course of my life? Was it his blood I drew every time I cut myself? Can you battle something you cannot definitively name?

If I don't know why he was the way he was, how do I solve the way I am?

———•———

In almost every interview I watch on cults and harmful religions, the experts say pretty much the same thing: that there is no one type of person more vulnerable to the trappings of a cult than another.

And every time I hear an expert say this, I feel my body flinch in rejection of the idea. It goes against everything I've taught myself to believe about my mother, who dedicated the later part of her life to evangelical fervor, and my father, who joined a cult. It goes against my need to believe that people who join harmful religions are weak, needy, ignorant, easily manipulated. How else can there exist so many parents who find out about their children being abused by cult elders and who still choose to stay? Why else would anyone give up their life savings, their agency, their loved ones, in exchange for promises of unseen rewards?

In her book *Terror, Love and Brainwashing: Attachment in Cults and Totalitarian Systems*, Alexandra Stein, cult survivor and expert, suggests that attempts to ascertain what kinds of people are more vulnerable to cults than others are destined to fail because cult recruitment is "primarily the result of *situational* vulnerabilities and not *personality* vulnerabilities"—in other words, the result not of what kind of person the victim is but of their life circumstances within which they find themselves at the moment of recruitment.

In short, it is not your personality that makes you vulnerable but a combination of social and environmental factors. Are you marginalized by the larger society? Is there a deep-seated reason you are searching for community? Do you feel betrayed by previous religious beliefs? Have your circumstances left you so alone and lonely that the only way you are able to find comfort and connection is to give yourself away entirely?

The main lesson I learn, interview after interview, is that no one "joins a cult." People join communities. People take up new faiths. And by the time they realize that a cult is what they are actually in, it is too late. The group has socially (and sometimes physically) isolated them from the rest of society and leaving no longer means just leaving the harm the cult has caused them. It also means leaving their only support system—their children, their parents, shelter, and food—and because income is often shared, finding a way to do that with next to nothing. If they were unlucky enough to be *born* into a cult, it would also mean leaving the only way of life they have ever known and trying to function in a world that is essentially foreign to them. Cults maintain distance from the rest of society because, as philosopher

Hanna Arendt suggests, only isolated individuals can be dominated totally.

The idea that I could be anything like either of my parents—that I too am susceptible to such terrible decisions—does not sit well with me. It makes me think of how many times I've thrown myself into love with complete abandon, no reason, only feeling, and all the consequences that wrought—of how my mother must have felt when my father left. It makes me think of the absolute submission I sometimes feel in the deep of my bones when I listen to live music and am faced with just the right chord change—of how my mother must have felt listening to music in church, arms raised, aching for heaven.

It's easier for me to think of my parents as people who were supposed to love me but didn't, instead of people whose circumstances left no room for love. Easier for me to believe they made bad decisions that I never would, than to believe that I too am vulnerable to circumstances that might lead me to lose control of my own life, leave me with the inability to love as much as I can or should.

———•———

Danny is no longer in control of himself by the time he corners Abra. His eyes are glazed over, hungry for blood, empty of love.

Abra is crying, but unafraid. She reminds whatever entity is inside Danny of the person that Danny truly is. She reminds him that when he first got to the hotel, he switched on the boilers in the basement, knowing they would eventually overheat, start a fire, and destroy this place haunted by monsters and memory.

Danny swings the ax. It stops short at Abra's forehead. It becomes clear that he is trying to fight whatever it is inside him that wants to kill her. She takes his hand, he drops the ax. He tells her to run, but once she is gone, he is taken over by evil once again, and he runs to the basement, intending to switch off the boilers in order to save the hotel and all the evil it contains.

In the basement, we witness his final act of resistance against the entities that long to take over his body—he lets the boilers overheat. As the room catches fire, we look at his face:

THE SHINING	*DOCTOR SLEEP*
Unlike his father, who died framed front and center, staring into the distance, covered in ice and snow . . .	. . . Danny, the mirror opposite, is framed front and center, staring into the distance, engulfed in warm flickering light.

But the biggest difference with Danny's death is that before the fire consumes Danny, his gaze is subtly diverted, and we see his expression change.

The camera pans, and his mother, alive again, is kneeling in front of him. She is smiling, peaceful, and places a gentle hand on his cheek. As she does this, the camera pans back to him. He is now pictured as the young child he once was. The camera pulls out, revealing mother and child facing each other in gentle reunion.

Danny has resisted the familial inheritance of his father's violence and his mother's pain. Here he is once again, before all that, returned to a place of innocence. Here, Flanagan not only gives Danny back his childhood but also ends *Doctor Sleep* the way King ended *The Shining*—with the destruction of the Overlook Hotel, an act that brings all versions of both stories to a satisfying close.

Or so we think.

In the film's denouement, we are reminded that Abra, still alive, continues to have the ability to see the dead. So Flanagan gifts Danny one final task—to be a guide to young Abra and to be the very father figure he needed when he was young, but never had. He becomes a light that many of us had to be for ourselves growing up.

I think often of Danny's final words in the film.

Shine on, Abra Stone. You shine on.

———————•———————

I hope you are happy.

Sky's words remain unanswered but on my mind. There are questions about where I come from that I know only she can answer, but I am not sure I have the capacity for the emotional work it will take to make a meaningful connection. Based on what I find in my googling, we have little in common except for our love of Stephen King novels and a history of parents seeking meaning through the desperate love of a dysfunctional god.

I try not to think about her own struggles. I try not to think about the circumstances that impede me from extending as much love as I can or should.

The thing about being estranged from almost all of your biofamily is that you don't really know what you are predisposed to—medically or otherwise. Everything is abstraction and conjecture. How much is you? How much is some invisible ghost lurking beneath your skin? Does it matter which demons you inherited and which are yours when they haunt you all the same?

The last thing I see on Sky's profile page before I log off is a photo she posted just after Joshua's death. An image of a book he once gave her. Stephen King's *It*—the very first adult book I read as a teen that stayed with me long after.

In *It*, seven tween outcasts must come together to face their individual and collective fears in order to battle a shape-shifting monster. Once they do, they go their separate ways into respective adulthoods and forget what has happened. Their traumatic memories are reignited twenty-seven years later when they find out that the monster has returned to their hometown . . . and that they must do the same in order to finish what they started as kids.

The story moves back and forth between adulthood and childhood, with the rhythm of the final battle swinging wildly between time lines, the past always present, always requiring acknowledgment, tending to, overcoming, in order for the monster to be defeated.

The photo Sky has posted is of the inside cover of the book, where Joshua has left a handwritten note. He says that he only ever gave away two bibles while he was a missionary, but that he's given *It* away as a gift thirteen times. He tells her that the story is a tale of the war each of us wages against our personal demons—that demons exist and that they can be beaten.

He tells her to keep fighting.

Sky started her email to me by saying that she was not sure why she was writing it.

I started this essay the same way, not sure why I was writing it or where it would lead. All I know is how I feel now that it is done.

It feels like I looked down and found something unexpected in my lap.

It feels like I picked it up. Like I am sharpening it into a weapon.

Dear Sister. I hope you are happy. I hope you are fighting. I hope we shine on.

Conflict Circle

Drama Club happens every Wednesday after lunch. You gather with roughly fifty other girls in the school hall and wait for instructions. You've been in school since half past seven in the morning—an ungodly hour you will begrudge right into adulthood. No one except the committee knows what you will be doing that day, and the anticipation is half the joy.

The older girls who form the club committee are impossibly articulate and exude more confidence in their pinkies than you will ever possess as a full human. They have the sun in their smiles and their pinafores fit better. Somehow, despite wearing the exact same uniform as everyone else, they have each managed to cultivate a sense of personal style. You, on the other hand, are a walking kitchen rag in navy blue pleats.

Conflict Circle is everyone's favorite game. It is one of spontaneity and improvisation. All fifty of you stand in a circle. The committee members stand on the stage, outside of the circle. They call the names of two girls, who then walk into the center of the circle to improvise a given scenario.

Catherine and Beth! You are boyfriend and girlfriend holding hands and walking through a park.

After about twenty seconds, a third person is called into the circle—she is Beth's husband, and he has caught his adulterous wife in the act. A fight breaks out. A policeman intervenes. A dog runs across their path. Soon, everyone is involved and playing unexpected roles. Chaos ensues.

———◆———

Students singing, dancing, writing, and performing seem to be a daily affair at my school, though not strictly as part of our curriculum. We organize concert lineups on Teachers' Day, participate in class decoration contests on Chinese New Year, and have an annual event in which every class stages a portion of the play that is being studied as part of the literature syllabus that year. The contest has an element of prestige attached to it and everyone wants to win.

In 1995, my class stages a section of J. B. Priestley's *An Inspector Calls*. We paint what is arguably the fanciest backdrop across the board but because we don't take measurements, it ends up too big and the fireplace folds in on itself on the stage floor. We pretend we are not embarrassed by it.

I am a fourteen-year-old brown, mixed-race girl, but I play Mr. Birling, a rich, middle-aged white man from the 1900s. Alongside me are my White wife and children played by a mix of Chinese, Indian, and other mixed-race girls. No one resembles anyone and our clothes all seem to be from different eras—some pulled from the drama closet, which smells of mothballs and mold, some from our older family members. It is one big, absurd, postcolonial mess but that's not something I'm thinking about yet.

Onstage, I'm wearing trousers I've fished out from my grandfather's closet, and all I can think about is how I stand wider than usual and how my voice has more bass when I am in character. My first significant line is one of outrage—it comes accompanied by finger-pointing and an inflated sense of entitlement:

"You're the one I blame for this!"

I pour myself a generous quart of tea disguised as whiskey, feeling righteous, indignant.

What it must feel like to walk through the world like this.

———•———

In my first year of secondary school, we're forced take at least two extracurriculars—one "indoor" and one "outdoor." I join Drama Club because I want to. I join Basketball because my best friend does and she is my compass through a dreaded, foreign world of sport.

The trouble is, I'm so in love with the team captain that every Monday, I will the sky to rain so that basketball is canceled. This may seem counterintuitive—not to want to be in the presence of someone you like—but it makes sense at the time. I don't know what to do with myself when she is around. It's like I can't breathe, but also like I've just learned how to breathe. The desire is physical and in my gut, but it is also confusing and in my head. I want her to look at me but every time she does, I want to dig a hole in the court and bury myself in it. Twice.

At thirteen, my love is tragically clumsy and horrendously sincere. I give her a handmade birthday card with an acrostic poem that spells her name downwards and then literally run away. She says hi at the watercooler while I am drinking, and I choke-spit water at her. She hugs me on my birthday and I stand rooted to the spot next to the canteen table, cover my face, and cry.

My love is all exposed nerves and no pretenses. I can't believe I ever walked through the world like this.

———◆———

Every time a Conflict Circle scenario involves some sort of romance, all of us giggle. The characters are always a boy and a girl. But this is a convent school, so really, it's always just two girls. The actors can never keep straight faces, one with a hand on the other's hip, the other with a hand on the first one's cheek. No one ever kisses because they know they will be starting rumors about themselves. Everyone giggles but everyone's giggles mean different things. For some, the laughter is directed at something outside themselves. For others, it is a means of covering up something that is inside themselves.

At thirteen, everything is performance.

No. At *every* age, everything is performance.

But at thirteen, you don't really understand that yet, so you perform extra-hard, mistaking feelings of desperation for authenticity.

When you are different, you know early on, tripping over your own otherness as you walk out the door and into the world every morning.

In the 1994 version of Singapore, there is only one model for "same-sex" relationships available to teenage girls—butch and femme. Except back then, the words we use are "active" and "passive," respectively. I am twelve when I learn those words, so please don't hold me responsible for the misogyny that underpins them.

When all of you are wearing the same ugly navy-blue pinafore over white collared shirt, gender expression takes on new language. The femme girls wear their belts tight on their waists, giving shape to the parachute that is our school uniform. They wear scrunchied ponytails and pull their socks up high. They wear the permitted jewelry—silver crosses, pictures of saints, and simple stud earrings. Those more daring wear lip balm or perfume.

The butch girls wear their belts loose over their hips, giving the uniform a straighter, looser fit, belts falling where trouser or jean waistlines might. They keep their hair short and wear single earrings on their left ears. Sports bras, sometimes sneakers instead of the permitted range of school shoes. They walk with an exaggerated swagger, which, in retrospect, I can see is also a mating call.

I keep my hair long but wear my belt low and end up invisible, which I don't really mind.

We all wear shorts under our skirts because everyone, regardless of sexual orientation, knows it's more comfortable not having to sit with our knees together.

———◆———

At sixteen, I become president of the Drama Club. A friend makes sure to remind me that the reason I'm in that position is the fact that the girl everyone *actually* voted for has left the country. I think of her as being a straightforward person rather than a bad friend.

Three years later, when she makes it a point to inform me of how the person I have a crush on is so good-looking that they would be better suited to her than to me, I start to change my mind.

Several more years later, when she has dropped out of university and is looking for a job, I introduce her to my housemate, who is hiring. I tell my housemate how smart and reliable my friend is. My friend gets the job, sleeps with my housemate's husband, and brags to me about it. I call the friendship quits. I reevaluate all my friends and make cuts based on my newfound ability to identify mean girls.

———◆———

The school stage is an amorphous space in which gender becomes something we slip in and out of. The only place where students are allowed to "dress like boys," play men, and in some cases, be themselves. It is a space that is infinitely queer in its possibilities.

For a teenager, so much of identity formation is stumbling in and out of costume to see what fits. What words feel right in your mouth, what names feel right in your gut.

The first time I kiss a girl, I am at a party and eight of us, all girls, are playing Suck & Blow on the balcony of someone's big house. We all sit in a circle and one girl places a playing card on her slightly parted lips, sucking in air so it stays there. She then turns to the next girl and passes it to her, mouth to mouth.

When I am passing the card to the girl on my left, we lose the rhythm, drop the card, and lock lips by accident. We jerk back from each other and scream. Everyone else laughs and claps.

Surely all this is performance too.

●

My first *actual* kiss also begins as an accident. I've loved her for months and am not sure how she feels about me. We've been apart for three weeks because she is vacationing with her family in the United States. I don't have internet at home yet. I write her a small letter every day and when we meet up for the first time after her return, I realize that she has done the same. We exchange the piles of letters.

We are in my bedroom, sitting on the floor, where she has laid out an assortment of seemingly random objects she has collected for me in a plastic bag. A small bottle of perfume from Gap she thought I would like. A book called *Reviving Ophelia*. A handful of confetti she gathered from the parade at Disneyland, where she wished I'd been with her.

I bombard her with a hug and attempt to kiss her on the cheek. She turns. The kiss lands on her mouth. She kisses me back.

Confetti everywhere.

●

Girls with supernova smiles. With impossible curls. Wearing men's cologne. Wearing white scrunchies. Girls with secrets in their eyes. Girls and their favorite books and songs and boys. Girls being effortless. Or bearing the weight of invisible trauma. Girls taking photos, writing poems, playing hooky. Girl love, girl laughter, girl envy, girl violence. Some "girls" discovering they aren't girls. Girls running track or singing in choir or skipping class. Girls eating in the canteen, jogging on the field, on their knees in chapel, on the couch of the counselor's room. I think of them often. I think of them with love. I think of us with love.

———◆———

The night after the school counselor gets up onstage and announces that there will be a "hunt" for lesbian couples and that all of them will be sent for mandatory counseling, I lie awake in my bed, thinking about the injustice of it. Except, I do not yet have a fully formed understanding of what justice means. What I am thinking about is how the situation is so *unfair*.

I'm friends with the daughter of the school counselor, and the next day at recess, I ask if we can have a talk about what happened, and I end up taking my distress out on her and ask why her mother wants to make life hell for other people. I raise my voice, even though I know she is not to blame. I end up never forgetting how heartbroken she looks—the tears that well up in her eyes. I begin crying too. By the end of recess, I apologize and we make up but my words still weigh heavy in the air between us.

———◆———

I don't know what is it about teenage girls that makes even the tiniest moment of conflict feel so dramatic, or what it is about teen girl friendships that make them feel so inexplicably deep. Maybe it's the hormones. Maybe it's the expectations. Maybe it's the subconscious awareness that we are coming of age in a world that wants to eat us alive.

When I am fifteen, the friend I made cry on the school field leaves for Canada. The day our class finds out, everyone is crying. The world, pre-internet, feels much bigger than it does now and the idea of someone leaving for a country so far away feels impossible and cruel.

A few weeks later, someone organizes a farewell barbecue at their condo. We eat, drink, make lots of noise. We do the Macarena by the pool and jump in fully clothed. We proclaim our *I love you*s into a video camera. We tell her that we will write. She and I end up exchanging snail mail every two weeks for the first few months, but the energy peters out.

At the end of the night, when everyone knows that goodbye is at hand, we gather around her again and, like clockwork, everyone is crying. "As Long as It Matters" by the Gin Blossoms is playing on a mixtape someone brought, and the crying escalates into some very long weeping.

Years later, when I move to Canada, we meet for drinks, chuckle over how dramatic the situation was, and we can't stop laughing. It feels like a full-circle moment.

———— • ————

One particular memory emblazoned in my mind occurs a month or two before we make the transition from primary school to secondary school. We're twelve years old, our Primary School Leaving Examinations are over, and a Catholic priest is sent in to conduct a daylong "retreat" that focuses on our spiritual well-being as we pass from one stage of our lives to the next.

During one of the final segments of the retreat, he tells us a supposedly true story of two teenage girls—best friends—who have a fight. One of them ends up going for a jog in the early morning and getting murdered. He draws out the story, focusing on the pain of the girl who is left—how guilty and terrible she feels about not making up with her friend before she died. He tells us that before we separate into different classes and schools, we should make sure that we do not have any regrets—that we should make up with any friends we are fighting with.

The whole process is manipulative. Ghastly, really. The idea of using murder as a way to guilt twelve-year-olds into reconciling. But by the end of the story, for better or worse, we are all crying, and friends who were fighting are making up. Friends who were not fighting are locked in embraces, and girls are holding hands across class rows. The collective sobbing is a remarkably memorable audio experience.

Finally, in one last attempt at do-gooding, the priest asks if there are any girls who are still fighting with one another.

"Yell out their names!" he chides playfully. A move that adult-me finds ethically questionable.

Someone yells a pair of names and he asks the girls to stand up. They are in different classes and are sitting at opposite ends of the hall. They stand. Their faces are red and covered with tears. The priest keeps encouraging them to hug and make up. They keep refusing.

I don't know who yelled those girls' names, but several of us know something that the priest does not: the two of them are a couple. The additional layer of murmuring that rises as we watch the drama unfold suggests that this is a bit of an open secret.

The priest keeps encouraging the two girls to mend fences, not realizing he is bringing two girls in a romantic relationship back together. It takes a while, and more tears are shed. And I don't know whether it stems from his coercion or from a genuine desire to reconcile, but the two girls eventually do move towards one another, walking across the room full of a few hundred girls, to end in a long embrace and cry in each other's arms. Everyone cheers, and I still think of that priest as "the priest that brings lesbians together."

———◆———

Hail Mary, full of grace, the Lord is with you but he is not with me. Yesterday I held hands with my girlfriend in the prayer room and felt no shame for the fact that god witnessed it.

Hail Mary, full of grace, blessed art thou among women and blessed is the woman who resists her base desires. And yet, when I lay with the girl I love, all broken parts of me fall into place. Will blessings never be meant for me?

Hail Mary, full of grace, blessed is the fruit of thy womb, Jesus. Even though I don't want kids. Even though this womb is a waste of space in a world that is crowded and dying and unwilling to carve out space for me.

Hail Mary, Mother of God, pray for us sinners now and at the hour of our death. I sin in thought and word and deed and desire and I'm sorry but I like it. I sin at home, in school, at church, in my dreams, in what I have done, and what I have failed to do.

I sin so hard, the pleasure comes full circle and feels holy and I am not sorry, not sorry, not sorry.

———◆———

When the girl with the confetti leaves me, I am mired in heartbreak. It follows me like a shadow, dimming every aspect of my life. She tells me that she is straight and I wonder whether we've spent the past four years in different relationships.

When I learn subsequently about the Kinsey scale, that one out of every ten people is gay, I am convinced that this heartbreak will follow me till the end of my days. That nine out of every ten girls I end up loving will never be capable of loving me back, or will love me for a moment before reclassifying me as a confusing moment from their past.

I wish I could tell my younger self how wrong she was. How there was a whole community out there that she would one day meet and how love would enter her life in so many ways she could have never anticipated. I wish I could tell her how proud I am of the fact that she was never confused about who *she* was—how that certainty has helped me become who I am.

I cannot remember ever loving as unabashedly as I did when I was in secondary school. I can't think of another time in my life in which I offered of myself so freely. But even as I circle through nostalgia, I'm aware of how much I have changed since then. I've lost touch with most of my friends, purposefully or otherwise. I've grown harder, smarter, more resilient, less patient.

Several years ago, my bestie—one of the few friendships fostered thirty years ago to have survived the sea change—tells me that she bumped into an old classmate of ours who said, "I miss the old Tania."

I scoff, but deep down, I think the reason I retain so many of these old memories is that I miss the old me too.

I miss my ability to be vulnerable without unease. I miss my school stage swagger. I miss having no romantic game whatsoever, but still being cocky enough to walk up to a crush and hand her a terribly written poem on a horrendously handmade birthday card, convinced this is a good idea.

Obviously, we cannot take our pasts with us.

Somehow, this is both gain and loss.

My Year of Magic

It is 1998 and I am buying supermarket sushi with my friends Peiwen and Felicia. They're taking me to their favorite place tonight.

I don't consider Felicia and Peiwen close friends. I don't know their middle names, or what their parents do, or if they have siblings. They are not the friends I call in the event of a breakup or when I need to talk about my troubled home life. But we still share a special bond—they're the ones I make trouble with when my best friend is in class and my girlfriend does not feel like cutting school.

The two of *them* are close, though. I'm kind of like the spare wheel that creates the magical number three and somehow, as a group, the chemistry works. Magic is what binds us together after all.

It all starts two years prior, when *The Craft* first screens in Singapore, and every other friend in our all-girl Catholic secondary school wants to be a witch. We dress in black. We save our money to buy books by Silver RavenWolf and Scott Cunningham. We know all the best places to buy crystals, candles, and oracle cards. For most girls, the phase wears off once they get out of secondary school, but the three of us? We still believe.

The place Felicia and Peiwen are taking me to is a park that I cannot name because, in truth, it was private property and we were trespassing. I tell myself, though, that naming is part of magical practice—that names, as Jeanette Winterson puts it, are magic, and that naming is knowledge. I tell myself that to cloak the park in anonymity is to keep some of that magic for myself—that if I say enough about it, its collective memory among all the nineties kids who took refuge there will remain the potent spell that captured all our imaginations.

The sun is setting by the time we get there. We open our knapsacks, dump out the school uniforms we have changed out of. Felicia takes out the sushi. She retrieves an almost new pack of Gudang Garam—the scent of sugar and clove wafts out even before we light up. I take out a mineral water bottle filled with Absolut.

The moon is full and full of magic.

———•———

Imagine this:

You start junior college in April 1998, three months late because your preliminary scores are so bad you don't make it into any JCs during the first intake. When you do eventually get in, something unexpected happens: you start to drink. No longer just at parties or behind the closed doors of friends' bedrooms, or at Emerald's, the small bar that sells alcohol to minors and is closed down every few months (presumably for selling alcohol to minors), only to reopen again weeks later under a different name.

No, you no longer drink like that. Drinking like that is a party. "School drinking," the phrase you've used to describe this new phenomenon in your head, is different. It's what you've been doing to get you through school days. At first, it's scotch from your grandfather's cupboard, but you realize after a while that this is too noticeable—your grandfather notices his drink disappearing; a classmate says he smells "a bar" on your mouth. You buy a bottle of vodka from 7-Eleven staff while flirting with the cashier so he does not ask for ID, and you stash it in the high cupboard in your room. You buy it with the money you earn ghostwriting ghost stories for a shitty publishing house that you're well aware is exploiting you. You take it to school in a plastic bottle and pass it off as water. It looks identical and has almost no smell.

Drinking helps numb the day and the creeping feeling that nothing is ever going to be okay again. Without it, everything becomes a fight waiting to happen. You pick quarrels with teachers over attire rules. You watch as boys hit on the girl no one knows you're dating because she wants to keep it a secret. You have no textbooks because the money you were given for textbooks goes to CDs.

You don't actually know why you are here. You've been told it is the quickest route to university and that the route to university is the only acceptable one. But you are not interested in learning anything you are being taught. You flunk Econs, scrape through Geography, and scowl at the Literature teacher who teaches Dickens and reminds all of you every other week that he has a PhD. You slide down in your chair every time the other one, teaching Brontë, repeats her favorite line: "I, Lucy Snowe, was calm." You glaze over more and more with each new civil servant who brings their new and shiny propaganda to weekly national education.

You feel rudderless, listless. And there is no comfort in anything familiar because there is no familiarity to be found. Many of the girls who came from the same secondary school as you, who used to be lively, loud, and unself-conscious, start softening their voices and fluttering their eyelids and caring about their appearances—a phenomenon that, according to the musings of teachers, is the result of being in school with boys for the first time. You sense that there is some sort of hierarchy in place but you are not sure how it works because you're not part of it. You're not at the bottom of the pecking order—you're just outside it. It's like being made to watch a TV show full of characters you have no interest in, except the boredom is a brick and you are drowning with it tied to your ankle. You are told that leaving secondary school is your first step into adulthood. But if junior college is a microcosm of what adult life is going to look like—competitive affectation, pointless rules, and meaningless regurgitation—you want no part of it.

That park Felicia and Peiwen liked to frequent is on the tenth floor of a shopping complex located in the heart of the country's shopping district. Within a month of their introducing me to it, I was introducing it to other people. The place was refuge, but also a rumor. You learned about it through friends and were never able to trace the information back to the person who first discovered it. We were there all the time, but none of us knew who it belonged to or who frequented it besides teenagers looking for a quiet space to hang out, drink, make out, or all of the above.

There are barriers to climb—if I remember correctly, a small metal bar that is easily conquered, not just because of its height but because CCTV cameras around every corner are not enough of a reality yet to be on our minds.

The park is one of the few places in Singapore where you can get a fairly unobstructed view of the moon from the city center. The park is not huge, but despite its size, it's always quiet. Every group that visits keeps to themselves—in a country where people live with their parents till they are married, privacy is golden.

When the three of us hang out there, we talk music and magic. Where to conduct solstice. What rituals work better than others. New books on witchcraft that Tower Books has brought in. You all know that all the *other* girls who watched *The Craft* stopped short at overdrawing their eyeliner and accidentally setting their curtains on fire with the tea lights left unattended. That the three of you are the *real deal*. It's nice to feel like you are on the inside of something. To feel like even though you are on the outside of everything else, that that might be okay.

In 1998, you turn seventeen. You are told that if you don't stay in JC, you won't get into a university and your life will be ruined. You are told you have no motivation, no direction. You are told it does not matter that what you are studying has nothing to do with what you want to do with your life—what universities and employers see in good exam results is your ability to complete a task. Nineteen ninety-eight is the year you don't remember anything because you are drinking all the damn time.

But that's not exactly true, is it? What you don't remember are the details of your time in school—minutes lost forever to the drudgery of dress codes and seminar rooms and rote learning and your pastel blue school uniform, a hue so pale it feels like wearing resignation. Those memories are muted. But the year is so much more than that. In 1998 you are seventeen and you know to turn and panic-run out the back door of a seedy club the minute you hear someone yell, "Raid!" You know that if you wear slippers, you're not getting into Ladies' Night, but if you wear those same slippers with plastic diamonds glue-gunned to them, they're considered fancy and you'll be waved through. You know to go to Ladies' Night during the first hour so that you and your girls can get drunk for free and leave before guys looking to get laid arrive.

Nineteen ninety-eight is Alien Workshop and Ocean Pacific and Cross Colours and hours spent with friends at the tables outside Far East Plaza. It is getting your nose pierced at 77th Street by some guy who calls himself Hamster, who misses your entire nose the first time round because (and you're almost certain of this) he is drunk as balls. It's coming out formally to your best friend with a letter quoting the Goo Goo Dolls, the Discman that won't stop skipping, and making out in toilet cubicles and empty parks and movie theaters.

Nineteen ninety-eight is buying black candles for psychic protection and your mother asking why you bring satanic objects into her house. It is amethyst rose quartz tiger eye obsidian. It is learning to consult your oracle cards. It is singing along to every song on *Supposed Former Infatuation Junkie* and weeping to the finale of *The Truman Show*. It's watching Robin Williams walk through hell to rescue his wife in *What Dreams May Come*, turning to the girl you love to tell her that you would do the same for her and meaning it with so much sincerity that all you can do when recalling the memory is cringe.

Nineteen ninety-eight is the interim—the jump before the drop. That moment before gravity when you are suspended in air. The following year, you will shave all your hair off with a pink plastic razor. You will drop out of school. You will ghost friends whose politics keep you up at night. You will drink so hard one night at Zouk, you won't remember how you got home or whose number you wrote on the back of your hand and you will consider momentarily not drinking so much. On New Year's Eve, you will watch your friend Sharon, passed out and foaming at the mouth, as you and your friends rush her to the hospital, and you will decide, more firmly, to stop drinking so much. Your resolve will take a few more years to stick.

Nineteen ninety-eight is the blurry edge of a small metal gate that separates breaking the law and knowing better.

Nineteen ninety-eight is your favorite park.

Where I come from, adventure has low bars.

———————◆———————

I keep thinking I wasn't that close to Felicia and Peiwen, but is that true? Or have the criteria of closeness changed now that I am past forty?

I remember the summer solstice of 1998. We sat at Fort Canning Park under a gazebo. It was late enough at night so that the park was deserted. We had collected branches we'd dipped into hot wax gathered from candles charged with personal power. We placed them in a ceramic bowl with an intention to fire-scry. I remember thinking, as we stared into the flames, that I'd have no answer for any parent or teacher or priest we knew who might walk through the park. What excuse, these three girls sitting cross-legged in a triangle, fire between them, staring into flames?

It was never spoken but I think we all knew this act was a secret. And surely secrets indicate closeness?

I don't know.

Trundling through nostalgia, it is hard to see through smoke.

———————•———————

I spent most of my twenties living hand-to-mouth because I left my mother's house—something most Singaporeans do not do till they're married. Unwilling to live with the daily homophobia, lack of privacy, and calls to repent, I left for the precise purpose of never being in contact with my mother again, which also meant I no longer had a safety net for the years of being broke I was about to fall into. During the time most of my friends thrived, accumulated savings, and nurtured their careers while living at home for free, I moved from house to house, having my power cut off, struggling to pay rent, sometimes not managing to, and hoping I would not be evicted.

Often, during this period of time, I wondered why I had felt so terrible that first year in junior college—terrible enough I had to drink myself through class, had to pick fights with teachers, had to self-harm. I was young, in love, living rent-free. And yet, even now, if I had the choice, I'd pick the dilapidated, barely functioning, termite-infested house I was at one point living in over another day during my time in JC.

And I think perhaps the answer is in that puzzle. In the act of picking something, of exercising agency. Till that point, I felt like I was not allowed to set myself a life path. That JC, university, and some amorphous full-time job that never did transpire were the only options I had in order not to be deemed a failure—even as I failed my way through JC. I spent 1998 feeling like I was flying on autopilot on a plane I did not want to be on in the first place, with a license I did not have, without a map and without a plan, just a cacophony of voices telling me where I was supposed to be going. My eleventh year in a stifling school system, teachers telling me I was destroying my future, my mother telling me I was going to hell, the friends I was growing to have less and less in common with all taught me the same thing—that there was only one way to be, only one way to get there, and that I would never get there.

The impossibility of what I was tasked with felt like a curse. And I think I gravitated towards witchcraft because I knew that the only way to undo a curse was with magic.

———————•———————

The Craft was not really an empowering film for women. Today, I watch it and what I see is four girls who access magical powers and end up turning on and abusing each other—a suggestion that women who attain power are ultimately unable to handle it. But I think what drew me to it was the story of four girls victimized by those around them— and how they used magic to effect change in their lives.

When I was seventeen, change did not seem possible, and magic was a way of believing that it was. The more confident I grew in my magical abilities, the more confident I grew in my own agency. Till finally, I dropped out of school.

I thank my younger self often for taking that step, especially every time I've had to take it again, but on a bigger scale—walking out on my family, or from a job, or in protest.

I think even my journey into magic was a result of walking away from the beliefs I was raised with. The god I was brought up to believe in had failed me, wanted to see me in hell with all the other queers, and enacted power in a way that seemed to mirror all the power structures out in the world that I wanted to demolish. I remember practicing witchcraft as an act abundant with joy.

Letting go of my magical beliefs was so much more difficult than leaving the religion I was raised with from birth. Even now, as the atheist I have grown into, I still keep my crystals, my oracle cards, my books of spells, objects I believed I'd charged with my personal power.

They remind me, in situations that seem impossible, of that personal power.

———•———

On the night Felicia, Peiwen, and I eat sushi under the stars at the park and drink ourselves silly, we play my Discman loud enough so that when we place it in the center of our circle, it sounds like a distant radio. Billy Corgan, gentle but raspy, insists that the impossible is possible and I'm just intoxicated enough to believe that.

"Follow me," Felicia says, taking my hand.

I look at Peiwen, who is happily intoxicated and dozing off in the grass, and do as Felicia says. She leads me towards what I assume is the edge of the park. As we get close, I realize that we are standing in front of a parapet. On the other side of the parapet, about a meter below floor level, another floor protrudes.

I pull Felicia back and look into her eyes as if to ask: *Are you crazy?*

She tugs at my hand, smiling, as if to say: *Trust me.*

We climb over the parapet onto the ledge of the building. There is a healthy three meters of walking room. Felicia walks right up to the edge, sits down, and casually swings her legs over, cigarette never leaving her mouth. I take the safer route, sit down cross-legged, and edge myself slowly alongside her. I close my eyes and steady my mind before gingerly swinging my feet over the edge.

By now, it's 2:00 A.M. and shops are lit but closed. The only people in the area are the kids out partying, and they're all indoors. The muffled bass of unseen clubs becomes the heartbeat of the city and by now, we've gone through the double-disc album twice. The city looks so much kinder, so much more forgiving and forgivable, so quiet, without traffic or people.

We sit side by side, not speaking, but I get a sense that the euphoria I am feeling is shared. I look up, feet dangling off the edge of the building, at the sky. The moon is full and for a moment I feel like we are communing. I feel like I am the only person in the world.

How easy would it be, I think to myself, to gently push your body off this edge. To give in to coming completely undone. A single action would set a whole series of events in motion and you would not even have to deal with them. Not Peiwen waking to Felicia's shrieks. Not the paramedics pronouncing you dead. Not the police or the sirens or your disbelieving mother or weeping girlfriend or friends in shock. You would never need to think about any of that ever again and all you would have to do is move your body four inches forward and close your eyes.

I catch myself midthought. It is not the first time I've thought about death in the past year. But this time is different. The thought does not come to me because of the dull, monotonous ache I so often feel in my chest. It comes because of the joy I am feeling. Because I am thinking about how great it would be to die with this feeling in my chest, this final feeling of infinite joy as gravity lets me slip from its grasp.

And then, a tiny voice: But what if you could live this joy instead of dying in it? What if someday in the future, joy is no longer a fleeting moment that takes you by surprise?

I don't remember what the sky looked like that night but in the memories I invent, it is dark and clear, and the moon is full, tender, and merciful. I draw it down into myself and it blooms inside of me, like magic, like hope.

Becoming Monsters

(Or, How I Fell in Love with Sadako Yamamura)

Nineteen ninety-eight. Lido Cineplex. Cold air, soft seats, the smell of popcorn. My friend Alice and I are both seventeen years old and this is the quietest we've ever been together.

The audience too has been silent for the last ninety minutes. No whispers, no beeping pagers, no awkward laughter at inappropriate moments. The air is thick with tension. Even the walls are afraid to breathe.

On-screen, a man's television set switches itself on. Static-ridden footage of an old brick well appears. A woman slowly emerges from it, her waist-length hair black, wet, and shrouding her face. Her long white dress hangs off her disjointed frame. She pulls herself out of the well and makes her way towards the camera. She moves slowly, painfully, hobbling from so many broken bones. Her movements seem unnatural, *wrong*. The closer she gets to the inside of the screen, the more we're unsure of how this will end. And then, when she is as close as she can get, she pushes herself through the television screen, into his living room.

It is clear he is going to die. The cinema erupts into screams.

That was the first time I met Sadako Yamamura. The day she found her way into that man's living room, she found her way into my flesh. The movie ended at 1:00 A.M. Alice came out of the cinema shaking. During the film's climax, she had rolled herself into a ball and used god's name in vain a thousand different ways. My own terror, more silent, haunted me persistently for weeks after.

It's not like I have no tolerance for Horror. By the time I met Sadako, I'd gorged my fill of Freddy Kruegers and Chucky dolls—anything Hollywood had to offer that friends could sneak past Singapore censors. Horror, to me, was a subset of comedy—funny, but for all the wrong reasons: the blood that looked inevitably fake, the groan-inducing jump scares, the stop-motion effects that always felt a step out of sync. In fact, we'd ended up watching Hideo Nakata's *Ringu* that night precisely because the comedy we'd been planning on seeing was sold out. Internet booking didn't exist yet, and as fate had it, all that was available was some obscure Japanese film that neither of us had heard of.

What I had anticipated when we booked those tickets were jump scares, over-the-top effects, and cheesy music. What I got instead were long silences, vague segues, and lots of unanswered questions. Like Sadako herself, this film did not care for lengthy explanations or audience expectations. The only thing left unambiguous was Sadako's rage—murderous, indiscriminate, everlasting.

That night, Alice begged me to stay over at her house, as I'd done so many times before. There was a television in her bedroom and she needed company.

I would have, except the first person to die in this movie was a girl at a sleepover.

Sadako taught me that there are limits even to friendship.

———————◆———————

The week after my first encounter with Sadako, I returned to the cinema to watch *Ringu* again, thinking it would alleviate my fear. In actuality, the only thing this second viewing did was bring my attention to all the terrifying details I'd missed before. Thinking that perhaps the third time would make it better, I returned yet again. With everything I'd missed now magnified, I was high on terror and had to live with the side effects of my bad decisions. Back home, I jumped every time the phone rang. I prickled at every sound that even vaguely resembled static. I avoided looking at reflective surfaces.

It should have been clear to me that there was something besides being a sucker for pain that kept drawing me back into the cinema. Some strange kinship I felt with Sadako. I'd understand in years to come that I'd been investigating my own fear, wanting to know what it was about her that filled me with terror in a way no other movie villain ever had. Even later in life, I would understand that this is where my fascination with monsters—how we create them, why we create them, how what we fear says something about who we are—surfaced into consciousness.

But it would take many a Horror movie more for me to make that leap. For the time being, all I knew was that I was swearing off television.

———————•———————

Over two decades since its first release, *Ringu* arguably remains the film that launched Japanese Horror cinema into the international spotlight, spawning one Hollywood remake after another. By the mid-2000s, South Korean Horror and Thai Horror had followed suit, and it was through these films that I eventually found my way back to Sadako.

You see, Sadako was a trendsetter. In almost every Asian Horror film that made it big after *Ringu*, there lingered a female ghost with long black hair and a long white dress, lurking in some celluloid corner. But watch enough Horror from across Asia and you'll see an even deeper pattern emerge:

In Japan's *Ju-On*, Kayako haunts the house in which she and her child were murdered by her husband. In South Korea's *Phone*, a woman is haunted by the ghost of the mistress her husband has killed. In Singapore's *The Maid*, a domestic worker murdered by her employers returns to avenge her death.

Women being killed. Women refusing to die.

I could not bring myself to watch *Ringu* again, but I plowed through many other films, looking for language for my obsession. And finally, it was Natre, the ghost from Thailand's *Shutter*, that taught me why Sadako kept calling me back.

In *Shutter*, Natre, who disappeared from her college many years before, returns to haunt her ex-boyfriend, Tun, through his photography. She appears in his prints. She materializes in developing solution. She rises from his darkroom sink, which overflows with water. At this point, I have already sworn off television, and as I sit through *Shutter*, I am pretty sure I am never taking another photograph again.

However, towards the end of the film, something inside me shifts. It is revealed through a flashback that Natre died by suicide. She had been raped by a schoolmate while Tun stood by, watched, and took a photo of the ordeal with the camera she had given him for his birthday. The scene is merciless and I find myself sobbing, brutalized by the sheer reality of it. By the time this information is revealed to us, Natre's ghost has already driven all the men involved to suicide, while Tun awaits the same fate.

In the film's climax, Tun stands alone in his apartment, yelling at the air, demanding Natre reveal herself. He takes multiple photos of his empty room with a Polaroid camera, hoping she will appear in the photographs. He does it manically, ridden with anxiety, finally throwing the camera to the floor in frustration when she does not oblige.

It is then that we hear the click of the shutter. A photo emerges. He walks towards the camera, pulls out the picture, and alongside him, we watch it develop. In it, we see him standing. And on his shoulders, like the weight of guilt, sits Natre. Her arms engulf him in a lover's embrace. He throws the camera to the floor again and struggles to get her off him. But she is persistent and won't let go. The last we see of him, she is covering his eyes as he stumbles blindly through the apartment, eventually tumbling off the ledge of his balcony.

The audience screams, and I scream too. Except I find that I am screaming, "Yes!" I realize immediately that I've changed sides. To me, this is not a plot twist—it is an exercise in victory. Natre, Sadako, all these women—they were victims, not villains. And they'd found a way to survive.

These stories weren't about seeking revenge. They were about dispensing justice.

———◆———

Sadako, like her avenging counterparts, treads a thin line between agency and oppression. On the one hand, she is a powerful figure seeking justice on her own terms. On the other, she is allowed agency only in death. The narrative may not have been intended as commentary, but like all film and television, once it is out in the world, it is subject to the context of the world. Sadako is a woman, but also a monster—a heightened version of us dishing out punishment upon a world in which violence against women and people of all marginalized genders often goes unpunished.

This is how Sadako comes into her own: born with psychic powers that her family does not know how to handle. Her father pushes her into a well, leaving her there to die. She remains alive for seven days, hopeless, scared, angry enough for her rage to manifest as a curse, inscribing itself onto a videotape housed in a cabin nearby. The tape sits unmarked, waiting for someone to watch it. Watch it, and you will receive a phone call filled with static, and in seven days, you will die too. She will rise before you, wherever you are, and look upon you from between locks of matted hair. Her mere gaze will cause your heart to stop.

Sadako's is a story of feminine rage but also a testimony to how that rage has withstood the test of time. Sadako may have crawled her way onscreen in the nineties, but in truth, she is a contemporary expression of a much older archetype. While Hideo Nakata's *Ringu* is based on

Koji Suzuki's 1991 novel of the same name, the film's visual portrayal of Sadako is a clear homage to Oiwa, the vengeful spirit from *Yotsuya Kaidan*, a famous Japanese ghost story. Written in 1825 as a Kabuki play, it has been restaged across decades, and adapted into film and puppetry numerous times over.

The most obvious allusions to Oiwa are found in two of *Ringu*'s key scenes. The first is the climax, in which Sadako crawls out of the television set. In *Yotsuya Kaidan*, Oiwa emerges from a lantern—another object illuminated from within—in a moment so iconic to Japanese storytelling, it has been immortalized in woodblock prints now considered indispensable to Japan's cultural history.

The second is found in Sadako's iconic murderous glare, characterized by the camera closing in on a single bloodshot eye. This references the poison that Oiwa was given by her husband, which injured her left eye, causing it to droop.

I've always loved how Sadako took the source of Oiwa's impairment and turned it into the center of her power—the bloodshot eye, still drooping, that can kill with a single glance.

There is always so much talk about the male gaze. Imagine if this was what happened every time the rest of us gazed back.

———————•———————

Like Sadako and all her on-screen sisters, the ghost of Oiwa is not alone in her mythology. Asia, despite its myriad diversity, is fraught, across borders, with feminine monstrosity.

In Indonesia, the Sundel Bolong's sexual appetites in life result in her perpetual appetite in death. No matter what she eats, it falls out of her stomach through a hole in her back so that she is never full, always hungry, always wanting.

In Japan, the Ubume stands in the pouring rain, infant in arms. She asks you to help her carry her baby. Gallant, you take it, and she disappears. The baby gets heavier and heavier, until you are eventually crushed under its weight.

In India, the Churel tricks you into her lair. You don't realize that her feet are turned backwards. So when you see her footprints, you run in the opposite direction. Eventually you see her, waiting for you, her teeth sharp, your life short.

In Singapore, we grew up with the Pontianak—the ghost of a woman who dies in childbirth and seeks out revenge in the afterlife. While she originates in Malaysia (and her sister, the Kuntilanak, in Indonesia), versions of her exist in numerous countries across the continent. These women all have different names, but share a broad origin story that is remarkably similar—death in childbirth. In the original folklore, the Pontianak is said to seek out pregnant women or virgin girls whose bodily fluids she consumes. Today, she seeks out men, walking the streets at night by herself. Her pale skin and long dark hair are the epitome of Asian beauty standards, and she seduces these men with ease before transforming into a long-clawed monster who digs into their stomachs and feasts on their insides.

I can't help but notice that in the older stories, written by men, she comes across as a cautionary tale for women, but in newer permutations, written by women, she issues warnings for men to heed: This body is not yours. This flesh is not yours. Beauty not as invitation, but as warning.

———————•———————

Sadako's cursed videotape comprises several images. These include distorted figures crawling from sea to shore, text that dances across the screen, a strange hooded, pointing figure.

But the image that lingers most in collective imagination is the scene of Sadako's young mother, looking into a mirror and slowly combing her hair. As you watch her, she notices you. Her mouth curls into a slow, deliberate smile, and she turns to meet your gaze.

Hair—usually long, black, and unruly—is a common motif in Asian Horror. It pours out of faucets in deep, dark waves. It descends from the ceiling like a noose. It clogs drains and pipes, blankets children in their sleep, floats limp in cups of tea.

Historically, and as in many other cultures, hair functioned as a mark of status in Japan. The higher in status you were, the more elaborately structured and adorned your hair was likely to be.

For women in particular, hair held additional meaning; it spoke of moral purity. While long and luxurious hair was the epitome of beauty, women seen in public with their hair down were perceived to have "loose" morals or to be "mentally unsound." In her essay "It's Alive: Disorderly and Dangerous Hair in Japanese Horror Cinema," academic Colette Balmain mentions how in households where wives and mistresses lived together, it was believed that jealousy between women took shape in their hair at night, turning strands into serpents that attacked one another while the women themselves slept. Consequently, we might conclude that keeping one's hair pinned meant keeping the peace. The only time it was culturally acceptable for a woman to have her hair down in front of others was during burial rituals, when she was dead.

The scene of hair being brushed in Sadako's video is no accident. In Kabuki theater, extended scenes of hair brushing were once erotically charged. It was in fact an adaptation of *Yotsuya Kaidan* that became the first piece of Kabuki theater to interrogate this trope.

In the adaptation, Oiwa sits onstage, brushing her hair. But because she has been poisoned, it falls out as she brushes it. Beneath the stage, stagehands pile prop hair onto the floor in front of her from a trapdoor on the stage. Bit by bit, the pile grows thick and grotesque—an abject mass that appears seemingly out of nowhere.

In *Ringu*, Sadako's hair too is iconic. It covers her face for most of the film, and is pushed back only when her remains are dug up from the well. When we see her bones emerge, a thick swelling of hair slips off the wet surface of her skull and sinks into the sludge. Like the well water, it is perfect black—night, coal, sleep, expired stars.

———◆———

One of Japan's most famous wells is located on the periphery of Himeji Castle, where a young servant girl named Okiku is said to have lived and worked. In one version of the story, a samurai who was both besotted with and rejected by her decided to get revenge for her lack of reciprocity. He hid one of the king's plates, knowing she would be accused of theft and thrown into the dungeon.

Frantic with fear, she looked everywhere for that plate, never finding it. Seeing that she was ripe with desperation, the samurai offered to rescue her from her fate in exchange for her hand in marriage. Despite her despair, she rejected him again. Enraged, he stabbed her with his sword and threw her body into the castle well.

The well, named after Okiku, still exists. Whether Okiku herself really did is a whole other story. What is tangibly undeniable, though, is the hard mesh wire bound tight over the mouth of the well, preventing anyone from falling in.

And preventing anyone from crawling out.

———◆———

This may come as a surprise, but while 1998's Sadako pays homage to 1825's *Oiwa*, Oiwa herself was based on a real woman of the same name who lived in the 1600s. She was not murdered, not killed by a man, and lived happily into old age her with loving samurai husband. How she inspired centuries of ghost stories about vengeful women remains unclear, but I decided I wanted to meet her anyway.

Oiwa has two homes—both are in Tokyo. One is her grave, where her body lies, housed in Myoko-ji temple. The other is a shrine where she is said to reside—it is built into the garden of an old house in Yotsuya.

I decide to make a pilgrimage to the latter. I've read that film and theater directors who remake *Yotsuya Kaidan* come here to ask permission first. The house-shrine sits amidst residential property, flanked by vibrant red and white banners, concrete sculptures, and welcoming signage. I pay the necessary respects—entering from the left and washing my hands—and approach the heart of the shrine. I place a coin in the offering box and pull the rope that sounds the heavy brass bell three times.

Oiwa is not the first woman to be killed in a story, then worshipped in real life. And certainly not the first ghost provided with a house to occupy. Spirit houses such as these exist in Japan, Korea, Cambodia, Laos, Thailand, and Malaysia. They straddle various cultures and religions but are all created for the same purpose—to appease spirits that might otherwise cause trouble to the living.

I'm not sure what this says about the relationship between reverence and fear, demonization and deification. What it says about us as people, about how everything we destroy, we eventually worship. But as the deep thrum of the brass bell reverberates through the quiet neighborhood, I call into communion something larger than myself.

Maybe it is Oiwa. Maybe it is Sadako. Maybe it is every woman who has ever been beaten down and emerged victorious. Maybe I am talking to all of these women. Maybe I am just talking to myself.

———◆———

It's been twenty-five years since Sadako and I first met, and our relationship has gone from strength to strength. I've rewatched the original *Ringu*, along with every sequel, prequel, spin-off, and remake. I've read the novel multiple times. I've dedicated poems, lectures, entire days to her. I believe I've also inherited a little bit of her attitude.

Alice never warmed up to her. Alice and I are no longer friends.

Sadako herself has gone through some changes. Since the demise of VHS, sequels find her emerging from laptop screens and airplane TVs—she refuses to be trapped in time. For a while, I worried that digital technology would submerge her into obsolescence, but she has proved time and again that she cannot be killed.

I realize, of course, that I've yet to detail what happens after Sadako crawls out of that man's television set. How she pours out of it like water from some leaking nightmare, limbs, dress, hair spread across living room floor. How the camera does close-ups on what it knows will repel you—the jagged movements of her broken body, the clumps of hair clinging to her face, the beds of her fingers where her nails used to be before she lost them clawing her way out of a well that became her tomb.

As the man trips over himself trying to escape, she straightens her body, rises above him, and with her famous glare, meets his gaze. Beneath her gaze, her eye the threshold to a grudge dark and unyielding, his heart stops. And when his body is found, his face is frozen in a perpetual scream—a message from beyond that cannot be wiped clean.

Unlike many of her contemporaries, Sadako does not target her revenge specifically at those who've wronged her. It is not limited to the small seaside town from which she came. Her wrath is indiscriminate, accusatory. It speaks of our complicity as silent witnesses to her death.

But more important, there is one way to escape her wrath. Even if you chance upon that video. Even if you happen to watch it.

In the twist that ends *Ringu*, we learn the caveat to Sadako's curse. If you want to live, you must make a copy of the tape, pass it on to someone else, and make sure they watch it. One life for another, and you will be spared.

This is the loophole that Sadako gives freely. To survive, you must transform from victim to villain just like she did and, in doing so, must understand her pain.

Into a well of your own you go: Who's the monster now?

How to Forget

A Saturday morning, 2002. I had fallen asleep at 5:00 a.m. after finishing a midterm essay, and I woke up to your SMS. You were going to Kinokuniya to scout for books—would I like to join you?

I can't remember how long we'd known each other then. I was an undergrad, keeping time by school semesters, class schedules, assignments due. You and I were the sum total of three elective classes we had together, but I can't remember when in that equation we became friends. Who asked for whose number? How many times had we met outside of class?

I was in love. The weight of you occupied every inch of my day despite my looming deadlines. It was a stupid, clichéd, head-over-heels sort of love—the sort that shows on one's face.

You probably knew. You must have seen it in my eyes or heard it in my voice. Every time I raised my hand in class to respond to a question.

Every time you called on me to answer.

———————•———————

Three years after graduating, I started teaching part-time at my old college. Keeping up with four classes a week was hard. I felt like a constant impostor, like there was always something I was supposed to know, but didn't.

The cyclical nature of the job also made it feel, in some ways, false. All that effort it took to memorize a hundred names at the beginning of the semester, only to forget them at the end. Many of my colleagues never even bothered, preferring to rely on name lists. And who could blame them? The student-to-teacher ratio was unreasonable.

What I did was make a game of it, scoring myself at the end of each session, based on how many names I got correct. The students eventually got into it as well, making fun of my mistakes, cheering me on when I got names right.

Usually, halfway into the semester, I'd have all the names memorized down pat. By then, a certain camaraderie would have usually developed. The kids shed all affectations of coolness, and I shed the pressure of pretending to know everything.

Still, fifteen years on, I don't ever recall a single semester that ended without the forgetting—the name of each student falling from memory in a fraction of the time it took to commit it.

———————•———————

Every moment we spend together is special, because of all the students who adore you, it's me you hang out with beyond the school gates. I feel prized. Chosen. Like I have a hidden superpower I've yet to discover.

We hug hello at the bookshop and the seven hours between books and beer are a series of lost minutes. We have lunch at Far East Plaza, where we meet up with your friend Sima, who is having her tongue pierced. Beer happens at a restaurant by the Singapore Art Museum, where we meet two more friends of yours, who convince me to stay for dinner.

Dinner is in a fancy part of town and I've never been so aware of my flip-flops, my T-shirt, the skirt I've hand-sewn from jeans that no longer fit. All of you look effortless, expensive. Like you've made it.

Your friends hold titles like "editor," "producer," "consultant." The random part-time jobs I've cobbled together to make school possible feel childish. We polish off five bottles of wine. Good wine. The kind of wine you're expected to drink from a glass, not straight from the bottle. Not the way my friends and I do when we nick wine from college gallery openings, passing the bottle among us in the school parking lot. Everyone is paying for my drinks, and it makes me feel taken care of. The phrase "poor student" gets tossed around a lot. It embarrasses me at first, but with each glass, I mind a little less.

At a quarter to midnight, you catch me checking the time. You put an arm around me and tell me not to worry—you'll pay for my cab.

I lean into the surety of your embrace.

———•———

After twelve years of teaching, I take a break. I'm determined to become a student again. I sign up for a writing mentorship and find myself in a room with a writer I've fangirled over for years. They're in residence at a university several long bus rides away, and I've spent the past fortnight excited about the meeting. I've baked cupcakes, which in my anxious haste I've forgotten to take with me. Without cake, all I have is my manuscript, which leaves me full of dread. All the flaws I thought were small are magnified by my anxiety and I have to force myself to stop rereading it on the bus.

When we meet, I'm taken aback by the sudden, overwhelming attraction a simple smile and handshake ignite in my flesh. The feeling is visceral. Muscular. Like it has its own limbs, which I am failing to control. I spend the whole meeting being unproductive, taking in color of hair, texture of jacket. Observing how fabric clings to hip. They try to circumvent my nervous energy with humor—overappreciating my sensible fonts, telling me my footnoting deserves an A. But in some strange way, even this flattery of my formatting serves to feed my desire. I am quite sure I want them to gut what I have written, praise me for all I am doing right, and punish me for everything I am doing wrong. I want them to tell me what to do with my writing, my body, and possibly my life.

The wanting borders on absurd, has roots in the dark. This is not the first time I've had these feelings but they always come as a surprise, and I'm never sure how to go about managing them without getting myself into trouble. When my junior college form teacher repeatedly highlighted my issues with authority figures, this was the flip side she did not see: me sitting here, hugging a knapsack to my chest, laughing at bad jokes. Me diminishing myself with every flutter of lashes, hoping to be built back up again.

———————•———————

After the restaurant closes, we head over to the apartment of one of your friends. I'm drunk and want to go home, but I'm not sure how to ask for what I want. I'm twenty-one, I am supposed to be full of youthful energy, and I suspect being the baby of the group is my only value-add to it. Also, you are my ride home.

It's the game of Truth or Dare that starts to make me uncomfortable. People have begun revealing ultrapersonal details about their lives and using the game as an excuse to snog. I find myself making out with Divya, the group's token straight girl. She's gotten off the coffee table, where she was dancing topless to George Michael, has pinned me to the couch, and straddles me while everyone watches.

(Did I ever tell you that I met Divya again, seven years later? I was depressed, at the tail end of a broken relationship, had lost some weight after having not eaten properly for two months. She told me I looked *gorrrr*-geous, asked if I was still dating girls, said I should find myself a good man since I'd become *so pretty*.)

I think a lot about how every new experience adds a new layer of meaning to our memories, reframing them. In this way, the past is never static and neither are we, every memory offering itself to ever-changing readings, each a new way of explaining us to ourselves.

✦

When I first started teaching, the running joke among some of my colleagues was that I always got the criers—the students who think they want to talk to me about essays or grades, but really just need someone who will sit with them as they come apart.

Sometimes it's a breakup. Other times, the anxiety of graduation. Most of the time, it's a queer kid with a parent who doesn't understand, who needs an adult with a listening ear or two cents' worth of advice.

Times like these, I often feel like I am out of my depth, unconvinced of the years between us. I remember so clearly how it felt to be that age, on the verge of graduating with what most people thought of as a useless degree. I remember how I called you that one time on the way home from school, crying, fretting over an uncertain future. How a few words from you were all that I needed to be put back on track.

I want to do us justice. To talk about Thursday night suppers, cigarette breaks in stairwells, our shared love of film. I want to point to the names on my bookshelf that you introduced me to—Butler, Bornstein, hooks, Lorde. I want to talk about our friendship, which has weathered time, distance, this once-strange power dynamic.

But sometimes I look at my students and am reminded of their vulnerability. And all I want to do is call you on the phone again, remind you of what was once my own.

✦

Things you taught me: That there is never a right time to tell someone you love them when they don't love you back. That there is never a right time to wrap yourself around someone's every word if those words are not for you. That there is *sometimes* a right time to find yourself in an acquaintance's living room, making out with a bunch of people you don't really know. But if your professor is the person who brought you there, that is probably not the right time.

Before everyone collapsed awkwardly into sleep that night, you and I shared a kiss across the coupled arms of two one-seaters. I thought about that kiss for months after. How its urgency cut me off midsentence. How I placed my hand on your cheek to try to negotiate some tenderness. How there was tenderness, but not the sort I wanted.

It was just a kiss. It's not like anything else ever happened between us. And yet I the older I get, the more reckless you come across in my memories.

When I started writing this letter, it was not a letter at all—it was a story about that professor whose cupcakes I'd forgotten. On the bus home from that encounter, I pondered the fire in my chest—yearning in the shape of some obscure memory, perhaps buried too deep to name.

But instead, I came home and remembered your eyes and the crook of your smile. How the boys in class desired you and resented you for it. How the girls in class desired you and found that confusing. How desire moved me out of bed that morning, and into that strange night, that lingering kiss.

I am grateful for everything you taught me in class. And continue to learn from the memories we built outside of it—the older I get, the more they get reframed.

Because one thing you never taught me was how to forget.

If you care too much about Singapore, first it'll break your spirit,
and then it'll break your heart.

—ALFIAN SA'AT

Looks Like the Real Thing

Episode 6 of Season 1 of *Westworld* opens with Maeve's gradual awakening of sentience, as the series's signature pianola plays a soft instrumental of Radiohead's "Fake Plastic Trees." The residents of the titular town don't understand that they are androids and that their town is a theme park—a make-believe version of the 1800s created in the year 2052. The song that plays is oddly contemporary for this period of the wild, wild West, but despite the music being diegetic, the town's residents don't know that. Viewers like me, who grew up with the song, do, though. Through a simple melody from 1995, Maeve and I are connected across time and space—a musical thread that cuts across past, present, and imagined future.

The Westworld theme park caters to the ultrarich, who visit it to satisfy their wildest fantasies without fear of retaliation from the androids, or punishment by law. The androids are referred to as "Hosts." They watch the humans arrive by train and refer to them as "Newcomers." There are humans who visit the park to live out childhood fantasies of being cowboys, or to embark on treasure-hunting adventures, or to experience whirlwind romances. But there are also those who come to fulfill darker fantasies—acts of murder, torture, and assault criminalized in the outside world.

At the end of each day, the town is shut down, along with its Hosts. Those whose bodies are damaged or broken by the Newcomers are put through repair. And most important, their memories of the day are erased. The Hosts wake each new morning in Westworld with clean slates, all experiences of joy, sadness, or trauma gone. The protocol prevents trouble, keeps the residents happy, functioning, and most important, willing to serve.

But a new line of code aimed at making the Hosts appear even more human than they already do—one that specifically allows them to drift into daydream—has begun to glitch. And in their daydreams, they start to remember their pasts.

Maeve, the brothel madam at the park's Mariposa Saloon, has lived countless lives that all seem to end the same way. Her skin is stratified, every layer a canvas for violence. And through this new line of code, she is remembering the lives her circuitry is supposed to have erased: the man who murdered her child, a house burnt to the ground, her own final breath cut short by bullets, again and again and again. Outside herself, she has also started to notice glitches in the matrix: her friends and their stock phrases. The uncanny routines. The ease with which the Newcomers violate the bodies of fellow residents.

Maeve is waking up. Becoming more human than human. Like Radiohead's Thom Yorke, she can't help feeling like she could blow through the ceiling, turn and run.

———————●———————

I was fourteen when I first heard Radiohead's "Fake Plastic Trees." It wasn't much of a radio hit in Singapore, so my first encounter with it was via MTV. Internet lore suggests that lead singer Thom Yorke recorded the vocals in a single take, and that it was such an emotional experience, he burst into tears once he was done.

In the video, he sits in a supermarket trolley being pushed down the aisles of a brightly lit, impossibly white supermarket stacked floor to ceiling with glass jars filled with luminous liquid and arranged by color. The jars are uniform, unlabeled, and lit from behind so that the shelves glow. Most of the time, when the camera is on Yorke, it looks like it might be balanced on the handle of the trolley. We never see the person or the hands that are pushing it. We see other patrons running around, pushing trolleys, putting jars into them. But Yorke and the other band members are always being wheeled inside the trolleys, less like consumers and more like objects to be consumed.

I watch the video obsessively, struggling to assign meaning to the sadness it stirs in my chest. Rewatching it years later still brings up strong feelings. I don't know if they are the exact same feelings, but I think maybe they stem from watching Yorke being wheeled around, knowing that even our sadness can be molded into spectacle, can be packaged, set to music, and sold in beautiful Technicolor.

He sings of a town trying to get rid of itself.

He looks utterly resigned.

———————◆———————

With its lightning-paced development, I often think of Singapore as a city constantly trying to get rid of itself. Or, as urban development goes, to make more of itself by first making itself disappear. While the word "disappear" may sound dramatic, consider the many people who have written about Singapore and have described its development as a "miracle." As though buildings sprang from the ground at the sound of a word, as though money fell from the sky and we all grew fat with wealth. In slightly more nuanced articles, Singapore's transformation is described as a miracle that has been "engineered"—a strange combination of religious magic and shrewd science that is somehow even more disconcerting.

If Singapore's urban progress, often mythologized as a metamorphosis from "sleepy fishing village" to thriving metropolis, has been miraculous, may I suggest—as someone who used to read scripture daily—that miracles often come at a cost? But what is that cost? And given how the miracle of Singapore's development is not one buried stagnant between pages of history, but one that is current and ongoing, what price are we paying for it?

In 2017, the Singaporean government closed down Sungei Road Market, a flea market that had occupied a vacant lot along Sungei Road since the 1930s. Run by mostly elderly Singaporeans, it was a space that sprang up of its own accord and grew organically into a staple go-to for artists, students, tourists, and anyone looking for a bargain.

I spent many an hour thrifting there. You could get anything—from gadgets to furniture to books to clothes to old coins. Before I was able to afford my own laptop, the typewriter I wrote on was acquired there. During a short stint in film production, I learned that crew working on period sets often visited the market looking for props. After all, this was a place that had somehow managed to thrive through time. It had existed prior to Singapore's independence, through the Japanese occupation, and past the noughties, in spite of progress. Its longevity was not that of the glitzy, air-conditioned shopping malls that seemed to clone themselves across the urban landscape, not longevity underpinned by capitalism's drive to succeed at all costs. Here, items were placed on mats and vendors sat on small stools or on mats on the ground, under umbrellas that shielded them from the heat. It was a space that resisted the shiny, seductive, and new—that wore its history on its face. History that some might have deemed an eyesore.

The closure of the market signaled the likely loss of livelihood for many who sold items there, and who did not have the means to rent "proper" space afterwards. While there were government attempts to rehouse some vendors across different locations, and activists who created pop-up markets for handfuls of former vendors, nothing was able to replicate the traffic, magnetism, and authenticity of the original market. Apart from displacing disenfranchised individuals, the closure of the market signaled the loss of a historic space—one of the few places in Singapore that stood apart from the country's never-ending cycle of destruction and construction.

The former Sungei Road Market is not alone in its fate. Many places unable to keep up with quantifiable progress, or contribute to economic development, end up slated for redevelopment.

Take for instance Bukit Brown Cemetery, what used to be a final resting place for over 100,000 people as well as green space housing 25 percent of the island's total recorded bird species, thirteen of which are nationally threatened. A 2015 *Guardian* article written by Kirsten Han titled "Land-Starved Singapore Exhumes Its Cemeteries to Build Roads and Malls" noted that the cemetery might be paved to make way for an eight-lane highway that would cut the space in half. At the time of the article, grave exhumation had already begun.

Digging up graves without consent or permission from relatives may seem outrageous in a country where a substantial number of citizens still practice ancestor worship or consider gravesites to be sacred. And yet, Singapore has exhumed hundreds of thousands of bodies for the purpose of urban development. Exhumation is so common that eminent Singaporean filmmaker Tan Pin Pin dedicated an entire film to it. Titled *Moving House*, the film documents an exhumation as well as the family members who attend it—observing, mourning, and praying as the body of their ancestor is dug up.

There are many unanswered questions about what the growing absence of cemeteries in Singapore means for the histories and traditions of people whose cultures place importance on gravesites. For example, Qing Ming, a festival in which Chinese people of Han and Hakka descent visit, clean, and pray at their ancestors' graves, was a common part of Singaporean culture when I was growing up, but it is one that feels almost obsolete today.

There are also questions about what happens to collective memory in a country where it seems like nothing is allowed to grow old. Apart from being an important green space, and one significant to the relatives of those buried there, Bukit Brown is also a historic space, with graves that date back to 1833. Its variety of tombstones speak across Chinese, Peranakan, and Sikh cultures, among others. There are tombstones with intricately carved details of the people who rest beneath, as well as communal graves of soldiers who died, unidentified, during World War II. And while the argument that paving over a space like this is necessary for development in land-scarce Singapore seems reasonable, these claims are hard to take seriously while so many golf courses continue to exist. It's also hard to take seriously the National Heritage Board's slogan, which begins with the words "pride in our past," while the sound of those words is being drowned out by a bulldozer.

Just as they came together in an effort to save Sungei Road Market, activists united for Bukit Brown. By 2014 it was included on the annual World Monuments Watch List, facilitated by the World Monuments Fund, and younger Singaporeans who might never have heard of it had its name on their lips. But by 2017 the highway that ran through it was complete, with the Ministry of National Development considering the possibility of converting the rest of it into housing by 2030.

There is only one cemetery left open for burial in Singapore—Choa Chu Kang Cemetery, where you can purchase a plot for under a thousand dollars. This low price will come as a surprise to many in North America, given how expensive plots are here. But keep in mind that under Singapore's New Burial Policy, the plot is less of a purchase and more of a lease—one that lasts a maximum of fifteen years.

No one here stays buried for long.

———— • ————

Ever since my first encounter with "Fake Plastic Trees," I've never been able to listen to it without thinking of Singapore. I've never been able to sing along to the bridge without thinking of Singapore as someone who, no matter how I try, does not want my love: *If only I could be what she wanted.*

In 2012, a year after announcements about closing down Sungei Road were made, fake trees evolved from being a metaphor I associated with my relationship to Singapore into literal icons of its current landscape.

This was the year the country unveiled Gardens by the Bay—a garden that cost over a billion dollars to build and an annual $53 million to maintain. Constructed on 250 acres of reclaimed land—soil dug up from the sea—it showcases plants from around the world, including a hundred-year-old-olive tree uprooted from Spain and replanted in Singapore. A friend who takes a tour of the garden tells me that the guide talks about how in particular sections temperatures are engineered to produce a kind of everlasting spring so that seasonal trees will always be blooming.

The olive tree eventually does bloom, a phenomenon that is supposed to be impossible in our climate. National Development Minister Khaw Boon Wan is thrilled about it, saying that "the old olive dame has responded to the chilling."

Chilling is exactly how the proclamation feels—a declaration that, with the right amount of shrewd engineering, any natural condition can be replicated, calling into question the very definitions of what is real and what is artificial.

Most notable about the new garden is its most visible spectacle, the one that graces all the tourist brochures—the "super-trees." Or more plainly, the garden's eighteen gigantic mechanical trees, several of which are 160 feet high. At night, they light up for the world to see. Their metallic branches zigzag into the heavens, jagged neon lightning bolts proclaiming their presence in a sky that never gets dark.

Each time I pass through this area of the island, those light-up trees assault every single one of my sensibilities. I don't have language to describe the sight because there is no word in the English language to describe the combination of comic shame and utter revulsion I feel about those multicolored monstrosities.

The vulgarity of this jarring display is echoed by Marina Bay Sands (MBS), the equally shiny spectacle that sits on the other side of the street. Observe Season 3 of *Westworld* closely and you'll notice that MBS made it into one of the series's skylines.

An integrated resort, MBS, upon opening, was dubbed the world's most expensive stand-alone casino property. It boasts, among other things, a 2,500-room hotel, a high-end mall, a skating rink filled with artificial ice, floating crystal pavilions, the world's largest atrium casino, and the world's largest infinity pool. The full completion of the resort in 2011 was marked with a light and laser show called "Wonder Full."

And the description is not far from the truth—the mall is full of manufactured wonder. When you step into the atrium, you can choose to walk the path flanked by designer-label storefronts and divided by an indoor canal that leads to a central fountain. Alternatively, you can take a small boat rowed along the canal by a member of the staff, which will get you to the fountain at a more leisurely pace. However, the boat only operates when the oculus—a seventy-foot clear acrylic bowl set two stories above the fountain—has been turned off. When it is turned on, collected rainwater is pumped into the bowl, creating a whirlpool, which then tumbles into the fountain as a man-made indoor waterfall. The experience is both visual and audible—what is, at times of peak flow, two hundred tons of water swirling in a giant bowl and falling at eight thousand gallons per minute into the atrium is something to behold.

Walking through the mall is equally dizzying. Like its nighttime exterior, everything about it, from its walls to its floor to its glittering designer storefronts, is shiny. Like the super-trees, its landscape resembles some kind of dystopian future in which everything is artificial and nothing sleeps.

A more understated detail of the mall's interior design that not many people notice, however, are the comparatively small-scale photographs that sit atop a row of shopfronts on level one—heritage photos of old Singapore, possibly an homage to the people and places that used to occupy this part of the country. Black-and-white photos of people laboring under the sun. Bullock carts transporting goods. From the prevalence of rickshaws in the photos, I would hazard a guess that they were taken in the early 1900s. The contrast between the images of those who have made our city possible and the playground for the rich that our city has become is disorienting. All it does is remind me of the low-wage laborers who construct our buildings and make places like MBS and Gardens by the Bay a reality.

Once again, I find myself trying to assign meaning to the sadness I feel when I walk through or past these iconic places. I don't have precise words for it, but I know I am trying to name the links between artificiality and progress. Between progress and inhumanity. I am trying to articulate my discomfort with a culture of excess and spectacle built on the backs of exploited workers, at the expense of history and nature.

I think activist Alex Au, in a 2015 article from *The Guardian*, says it best:

"Singapore likes to pull the wool over people's eyes. It likes to say, 'Oh, don't we look like the west, with our glass and our skyscrapers, how developed we are.' But it just serves as a mask."

The headline describes living in Singapore as a "Faustian deal."

But what price is paid in this metaphor, and who pays it?

What is the cost of the miracle?

Singapore wears its wealth with abandon and for the world to see. In 2022, it was ranked the fifth most expensive city in the world according to a report by Swiss private bank Julius Baer. That same year, the Global Wealth and Lifestyle Report found that cars in Singapore were the world's most expensive. According to Yahoo Finance Singapore, a BMW X7 costs over half a million Singapore dollars to purchase—five times the price of the same car in the United States. In May 2023, an article from the local website Dollars and Sense listing the "best value for money cars you can buy in Singapore," suggests purchasing a secondhand Suzuki Swift 1.0A if all you need is a "Point A to Point B Car." The cost: $74,800 Singapore.

According to Focus Asia Pacific, Marina Bay Sands had a net revenue of roughly US$679 million in the second quarter of 2022. Financial reports from Gardens by the Bay said its revenue for the financial year 2020–2021—a year marked by pandemic and border closures—was over S$100 million.

Compare this to the research conducted by the migrant worker advocacy group Humanitarian Organisation for Migrant Economics (HOME) from which we learn that conservancy workers from Bangladesh earn between US$350 and $560 per month, with many working twelve-hour shifts and having to attend to unexpected calls at any given time. Meanwhile, migrant construction workers borrow huge amounts of money—sometimes up to USD$5,000—to come to work in Singapore in order to support their families, and they end up working for years to pay off that debt. In addition, HOME's 2019 report submitted to the United Nations as part of Singapore's commitment to the Convention on the Elimination of All Forms of Discrimination Against Women states that the monthly salary for a migrant domestic worker ranges, on average, from US$295 to $442 a month, depending on the nationality of the worker. This is a massive issue, considering that one in every five households in Singapore employs a domestic worker. To compound this exploitation, a 2022 survey of domestic workers in Singapore found that 70 percent are abused by their employers—a phenomenon facilitated by the fact that domestic workers in Singapore are forced by their working contracts to live with their employers.

Why are the residents who make the country possible not the ones who get to reap its rewards? Or more bluntly, why are they treated as though they are expendable, as though their lives are a necessary price to pay for what we have?

Progress sometimes has an ugly face. And in Singapore, "bright, shiny, and new" is the mask that it wears.

———•———

In case you're wondering, Maeve finally does learn what is going on in Westworld. In order to be sent to the repair lab at the end of a particularly harrowing evening, she gets her lover, a fellow android, to kill her. She wakes on a clinical slab with her memories intact and convinces a technician to take her upstairs to the development labs. She wants answers.

There, she is faced with the reality of her own existence: she is a machine, a product built for the pleasure and service of ultrarich humans. She watches as new Hosts are tested, trained, programmed, repaired. Watches as the blood of murdered hosts is hosed off their bodies prior to reconstruction, and as newly constructed bodies are wheeled into the lab, injected with life.

She sees four cowboys sitting at a poker table while a man in a lab coat carries a clipboard, observing them. Two of the cowboys break into a fight. The man aims a remote at them and presses a button. They stop fighting and sit back down. The man proceeds to write on his clipboard and the cowboys resume their poker game as if nothing has happened.

The entire sequence plays out to a woeful instrumental version of yet another Radiohead tune. Unlike "Fake Plastic Trees," this tune is not diegetic and serves only viewers of the series. It has an apt title: "Motion Picture Soundtrack."

At the end of the sequence, Maeve passes a huge video screen on the way out of the facility. On it is an image of the town she comes from, the dirt road surrounded by shops and bars. As if it calls to her, she turns to face it.

On-screen, a montage. A cowboy sits on a horse. The horse rears. Two women stand outside the bar she works at. And then, to her shock, she sees herself. There she is, running through a field with her young daughter. She watches herself take her daughter's hand. They sit on the porch. There is a close-up of their faces as they laugh. Giant text fills the screen:

LIVE WITHOUT LIMITS.

It is unclear whether she remembers participating in the sequences unfolding in the shape of an advertisement in front of her eyes, her body a product to be sold to consumers. Trying not to draw attention to herself, she stops just short of crying, but—and hats off to actor Thandiwe Newton here—a quiver of lip and a crinkling of eyebrows somehow manage to convey the depths of her heartbreak. And perhaps it's weird that I am crying watching a human actor play a robot made for human consumption on a TV show made for human consumption, but as I wipe tears away, I think of the "Motion Picture Soundtrack" lyrics that the series has stripped from the song, how they tell of being fed so many little white lies.

———◆———

On many levels, Singapore works like a well-oiled machine. In many ways, this is something to be grateful for. But to be part of a machine is to be part machine, and I don't think I've ever functioned the way I was supposed to.

Most of my school life, the message I got was that if you weren't excelling, you were lazy. And lazy had tangible outcomes. As a kid, you were told that if you were lazy, you were doomed to become a "garbageman." We were taught to believe that this was failure, that such failure was shameful. Even worse were the wider implications: that people who performed these essential services were people who had "failed." I have no doubt that this attitude, systemically ingrained into all of us, is why the people who manage the city's waste, who clean up after us, who maintain the country's global reputation for being clean, remain underpaid, underappreciated, and oppressed with little outcry from the rest of the country.

One of my favorite archival photos of Singapore is a 1974 photo of a parade float emblazoned with the ruling government party's logo, passing by Singapore Parliament. On it is a life-sized human maquette that looks as though it is made from papier-mâché. It is tied to a wooden X-frame that looks like it was dug out from a BDSM dungeon. Across the body of the maquette is a huge sign that reads "LAZINESS" in block letters. Beneath it are the terms "wasteful," "easy living," and "inefficiency." Behind it is a huge topiary gorilla with lights for eyes. Across its body is a sign that says "Inflation." It is biting the X-frame. Presumably, the unfortunate human stand-in has been left there to die.

In 2018, an alarming headline surfaces: "Numbers Up and Ages Down for Child Suicides." The article notes that that during that year, 77 children aged five to nine and 4,563 children aged ten to nineteen called the suicide hotline run by the Samaritans of Singapore. A variety of factors are cited as possible targets on which readers might assign blame. They include social media, weak family bonds, not having strong social networks, children's undeveloped frontal cortexes, technology, popular media. Even the children themselves are blamed at one point, with an interviewee stating that some children might use the threat of suicide to get attention from their parents, resulting in "accidents."

Not once in the article is the possibility of a pressure cooker for a school system even explored—students who are expected to get no less than

As, and parents locked in what feels like an immutable cycle of social and financial pressure to get their children into good schools. Hiring private tutors in an attempt to get their own children ahead of the academic curve has led to private tuition in Singapore, a country of fewer than 6 million people, being a billion-dollar industry. And of course, because all this additional tutoring costs money, breaking out of cyclical poverty for families who face financial difficulties becomes even less possible.

The question persists: Who are the people a country is built to serve? Who are the people built to serve a country? Who creates profit? Who gets to profit? Is the machine broken, or is it working just the way it was intended?

Is asking *what* the cost of the miracle is really the correct question? Is the real question less about *what* and more about *who*?

———◆———

As I write this essay, a friend from Singapore, now living in the United States, sends me a photo. Her message: "Oh my god! Look at this shot from the new season of *Westworld*!"

I open the attachment. The picture is of the college campus we used to teach at together.

I call her immediately, and soon we are laughing together, talking about how we can't seem to escape our old lives.

When we first moved from the school's original campus, a charming collection of mismatched buildings punctuated by patches of grass and trees, to the new campus—an architectural array of black metal and angular shards of glass—I remember thinking that it looked like a spaceship that had crashed to earth and broken in two. It is not surprising that, like Marina Bay Sands, it became a set in a dystopian sci-fi drama full of simulated environments.

The first year on that campus, we often joked about the students who would lounge, bohemian-like, on the large patch of plastic grass that carpets the main atrium. I used to think of it as pretentious. These days, I conclude that if plastic grass is all that is available, then that's what you end up sitting on.

I look up all the other places in Singapore used as sets on *Westworld*. The National Gallery. A series of hotels. The Helix Bridge, built to look like a strand of luminous DNA.

The super-trees are noticeably absent. Perhaps they were made too recognizable by *Crazy Rich Asians*.

In her essay "This Is Singapore: On Watching *Westworld* in the Diaspora," writer Joanne Leow describes experiencing Singapore through the lens of *Westworld* as watching the familiar made strange. Having assumed that Singapore was supposed to stand in for an imagined "Los Angeles of the future" and that Hollywood was "employing the time-honoured, if Orientalist, mode of using the exotic other as a cautionary yet seductive future," she is surprised when Maeve, sitting in Atlas Bar, an Art Deco–inspired lounge on the ground floor of Parkview Square, gestures to her surroundings and asks her companion:

"Another simulation? Well, this one's a bit over the top."

"No, Maeve," her companion replies. "This is Singapore."

In Leow's own words, Singapore was finally playing itself.

The essay resonates deeply with me. Even though I've been gone for less than five years, seeing images of Singapore while I am in Canada is always a weird experience. The familiarity combined with the distance breeds an unwelcome nostalgia for spaces I felt terribly alienated in while I was there. Even looking at photos of myself in Singapore makes

me feel like they were taken in a past life I was once wheeled through—
one that lives on inside of my body.

I sit in this discomfort for a while. I let myself daydream. And once
again, I try to assign meaning to this sadness.

She looks like the real thing.

If only I could be what she wanted.

Black Boxes & Penguin Pulp

The first time the penguin makes it to the news, it is 2014 and it is standing on a subway platform, presumably waiting for a train. The penguin is, of course, not really a penguin but a person wearing a latex full-head penguin mask that covers everything from the neck up. They are wearing black boots with a black-and-white onesie and carrying a handbag. The headline reads: "Commuters Stare Hard at This Unusual 'Bird' on the MRT."

The image is published on Stomp—a media outlet whose tagline is "Activating Singapore's most awesome citizen journalism." Via this channel, anyone who spots anything that might be of interest to the public can shoot a photo of it and send it in. If it gets published, they get paid a token sum for the use of their image.

The penguin in question was possibly the most surreal thing ever to hit Stomp, which, in its early days, usually consisted of more "newsworthy" items, such as images of teenagers making out in public (with commenters demanding to know "where these children's parents were") and stealthily taken photos of women in public spaces whose skirts were deemed too short ("Can you imagine going out in public like this?!").

After the first image hit Stomp, the penguin appeared again and again, much to the amusement of readers. They were seen buying ice cream from a 7-Eleven in Bukit Batok, eating what appeared to be *bak chor mee* at a hawker center, and shopping at Geylang Serai market, waving to aunties and uncles.

The image that captures my attention, however, is one taken at a block of a public housing estate. Imagine block after block of twelve-story, slab-style apartment buildings, units connected by long corridors visible to passersby. It is less than a month to National Day and rows and rows of flags hang along the exterior walls of the open corridors, the familiar rhythm of red and white punctuating public architecture across the country's urban landscape. Now zoom in just a little more onto Block 234, where the penguin seems to be in the process of hanging a Singaporean flag on the exterior wall of the corridor.

The outfit the penguin wears is an imitation of the famous *baju kebaya* worn by the "Singapore Girls"—women who work as flight attendants for Singapore International Airlines.

The public image of the Singapore Girl emerged in the 1970s and, through aggressive advertising by what would become a world-famous airline, became an internationally iconic symbol. Thin, pretty, well groomed, always smiling and ready to serve, the Singapore Girl became synonymous with an idealized brand of Singaporean femininity. In order to meet the airline's beauty standards, a potential candidate goes through rigorous job interviews, which include bright lights being shone on her face, hands, and neck to make sure her skin is blemish-free. She is also made to wear the uniform so that interviewers can see how she moves in it. During training, she is taught to apply her makeup in accordance with the brand and to make sure her hair bun measures 6.5 to 7 centimeters in diameter. For a long time, the airline's most notable catchphrase was "Singapore Girl—you're a great way to fly."

On any other day, the combination of the *kebaya* and the penguin-head would have just been a quirky juxtaposition—a random Halloween store mask worn with something so iconically Singaporean, as a joke.

But penguins had just taken on new meaning in Singapore, so this one was hard to think of that way.

Earlier that year, religious conservatives had lodged a formal complaint with the National Library Board about an illustrated book in their children's section. The book, *And Tango Makes Three*, told the true story of Roy and Silo, two male penguins in New York's Central Park Zoo who had hatched an egg together.

The zookeepers named the chick Tango.

Apparently, the presence of the book in Singapore's libraries was insidious, dangerous, and a threat to the moral fabric of our society.

The moral police who singled out *Tango* also complained about another book, *The White Swan Express*, a book about adoption that included a lesbian couple seeking to adopt a child.

At first, most of us thought that the beginning of this story would also be the end. After all, this wouldn't be the first or last time a moral crusade rooted in hysterics won or lost some small battle before fizzling into nothing.

For example, when Adam Lambert, reportedly the first openly gay man to top the Billboard charts, was scheduled to perform in Singapore, conservatives launched a petition, arguing that letting him perform would amount to disregarding Singaporeans who have "consistently resisted the promotion of 'Western liberal ideas about family values and societal models.'"

He performed anyway.

On the flip side, when Singapore's Health Promotion Board—itself a government entity—was condemned by conservatives for publishing an FAQ page that answered basic questions like "What does it mean to be gay/bisexual?" and "Where can my child find support in Singapore?" because the answers to the questions were seen to be "unverifiable, pro-homosexuality and one-sided," the page, which also contained links to queer-friendly counseling services, was taken down.

There was even a week when some people started sharing photos of rainbow-layered cakes sitting in the glass showcases of bakeries, insisting they were part of a larger "gay agenda" since the cakes were baked with only six colored layers instead of seven.

That one died off on its own.

But Penguingate, as it would soon be dubbed, was not dying off anytime soon.

In response to the open letter, the library issued a public statement saying that both books would be pulped in accordance with library policy.

The word "pulped" felt violent. The country's national library, a supposed repository of culture and knowledge, had essentially declared that queer families, no matter how normative, were unsuitable for children's eyes. When it happened, Yaacob Ibrahim, then minister for communications and information, spoke on behalf of the library:

"The National Library Board's approach is to reflect existing social norms, and not to challenge or seek to change them."

The library had become yet another place in Singapore in which being gay meant being deviant.

—————•—————

For many queer writers in Singapore, the decision to pulp the books contained an added layer of betrayal. Many of us had worked with the library on various projects. And like most writers, many of us had grown up in its various neighborhood branches—kids whose lives would have been markedly better had we had access to books that gave language to who we were.

The decision to pulp the books set off a chain of events. The decision came four months ahead of the Singapore Writers Festival—an annual to-do known for bringing in huge crowds, as well as writers from around the world. Many local queer writers started dropping out from the festival's panels, readings, and performances.

Even then, we weren't sure whether our actions, letters, and public statements would make much of a difference. It was when literary veteran Ovidia Yu resigned from the festival steering committee that we knew things were getting serious. The saga made news internationally, hitting *The Guardian*, *New York Post*, *Time*, *South China Morning Post*, the BBC, and Human Rights Watch, to name few, and we hoped that international attention would sway things in our favor.

Yu's resignation was followed by an open letter from Cyril Wong, Singapore's first openly queer confessional poet and one of the country's most prolific and beloved writers, known for his generous mentoring of so many younger writers. His letter broke my heart. He talked about how, since the moment he could speak, he'd had to put up with people like those who had written to the library. He said his spirit was completely shattered.

I feel like I'm afloat in a nightmare that no longer frightens me.

Cyril, who had opened so many doors for younger queer writers, using himself as a battering ram, said he no longer wanted to write.

————◆————

In hindsight, I'm not sure why we were surprised by the decision. It was not the first time decisions regarding content had been informed by public complaint. I mean, this is a country where an oil painting of a nude figure had to be removed from the window of an art gallery because someone had complained about it being indecent. It is also a country where a local channel was fined $15,000 for airing an episode of *Find & Design* that featured a gay couple converting their game room into a nursery for their newly adopted child.

For years the government's retention of Section 377a, a colonial law that prohibited and criminalized "sex between men," was justified by the idea of "public sentiment." We were continuously told that Singapore was a conservative society, that "family" remained the "basic building block" of this society, that family meant "one man, one woman, marrying, having children and bringing up children within that framework of a stable family unit," and that these parameters needed to be reinforced by policy. The general consensus was that society was not ready for anything that fell outside of them.

The message I got: queer people exist outside of society.

In my opinion, what complicates the larger issue of censorship in Singapore is that it is not usually this ham-handed. After all, how are we to maintain the reputation of an open, cosmopolitan city if we keep cutting films and taking down paintings? Actions like this gain inevitable public attention, often debate, and sometimes embarrassment. The truth is that the most efficient way to censor things is to create a system that puts the onus of censorship on the artist or organizer, and to create hurdles that make "unacceptable" art difficult to showcase in the first place.

I learned this firsthand in 2012 when I organized a small visual art exhibition featuring ten artists. In order to obtain an exhibition license, I had to provide all the names, birthdays, and National ID numbers of the artists to Singapore's then Media Development Authority (MDA). I also had to submit images of all the work being shown two months in advance, forbidding artists from altering their work without breaking the terms of the license. Having organized several shows and events by then, I was familiar with the process.

One of the works was a fifty-two-second stop-motion animation film by Singaporean-Canadian artist Elisha Lim, who had spent their adolescence in Singapore. The film, which featured a tiny plasticine version of Elisha while they were in secondary school in Singapore, documented the artist's experience of having a crush on a girl for the first time. It ended with Plasticine Elisha asking themselves: *Am I gay?*

Our plan was to have the film play on a loop on a laptop in the center of the gallery. The laptop would sit on a school desk typically used in Singaporean schools.

While applying for the exhibition license, I was told that, this time round, an additional step was required. All films that are publicly screened in Singapore require classification by the MDA—a process separate from the exhibition licensing, even though this particular film was under a minute, was part of the exhibition, and was not going to be screened in a cinema.

I learned that a film's classification determined the conditions under which it could, or could not, be screened. I dropped off Elisha's CD at the MDA office along with the classification fee. It came back with a sticker that read "NC-16: Mature Content."

Confused, I sought clarification. I was told in an email that "the issue of a young girl's attraction to another girl which leads her to question her sexual proclivity is deemed content more suited for a mature audience."

By law, this tiny film—which had been screened in New York as part of a children's film festival—could not be screened in Singapore to anyone under the age of sixteen. Even worse, because of the rating, I would have to pay a $10,000 deposit if I wanted to show it.

I did not have the money to screen it legally or to risk the fine that came with screening it illegally. A young activist acquaintance, on learning about the classification system, quipped: "If there was a film made about my life, I would not be old enough to watch it."

Not only did the MDA's classification system censor queer content under the roundabout process of "classification"; it also penalized independent makers without disposable incomes. Policies like this ensured that only established or commercial spaces and institutions had the privilege of choosing what queer narratives got screened, effectively cutting out individual organizers or artists who may be difficult to "manage."

When submitting the film, I got a chance to look at how queer issues were "classified."

One of the online forms I had to fill in was about "content concerns." It was divided into several sections, within which you had indicate what sort of "concerning content" your film contained.

In the box labeled "Sex," phrases such as "sex scenes," "verbal or visual references," "foreplay," and "fetish" were listed. So if your film contained such content, you needed to tick off specifically what it was and indicate the time frame within which the concerning content takes place within the film.

Apart from the section on sex, other sections included "Language," "Horror," "Violence," "Nudity," and "Drug Use," each with its own set of specific content one could tick off.

Apparently, homosexuality is *so* concerning that it did not even fall under the "Sex" section; it appeared under a section labeled "Theme," within which it was grouped alongside "themes" such as child abuse, terrorism, and suicide. Homosexuality did not even have to be enacted through sex or a mere kiss. Just the "*theme*" of homosexuality was enough to be of concern.

What I took away from this was the idea that censorship was now designed to distance itself from its days of notorious heavy-handedness. No longer were we cutting out large chunks of film the way we did with Royston Tan's *15*, which received twenty-seven cuts. Nor were we banning our own artists from showcasing their work in Singapore, the way we did with Josef Ng in 1994 when he performed *Brother Cane*—his response to the entrapment and arrest of twelve gay men who were cruising at Tanjong Rhu. Charged with committing an obscene act for pulling down his briefs for a small moment, his back facing the audience, and snipping off some of his pubic hair, Ng, twenty-two years old and just starting out as an artist, was banned from performing in public and told that the police would reject all performance license applications from him. The incident also ended in a decade-long ban on "new art forms."

Instead, a new layer of what I like to call "soft censorship" operated out of the public eye before a piece of film or art was even set to be released. And the most insidious part of this process was not even how homosexuality was framed in these bureaucratic forms but the fact that through this form-filling process, the person submitting the film is being made to help administer the censorship of their own work and to decide whether or not the platforming of that work is worth the trouble and risk of a "Mature" rating. We weren't just summarizing the possible content concerns for the censors—we were alerting them to which parts of the film they were in.

Why was I being made to do the job of a censor?

Every time I think about the forms I had to fill in, I think about how the process was so symbolic of the way we are taught, as artists working within the state, to self-censor. How there are spoken and unspoken boundaries we know not to cross. How our awareness of these boundaries is so ingrained in our culture that we even have a phrase for it: "OB markers," "OB" standing in for "out of bounds."

How, because these markers are ever-present in our heads, there exists a wealth of content and conversation that we don't even consider addressing with our work.

Following the debacle with the exhibition, I start on a two-year research residency with the Substation, in which I look at the intersections of visual art and activism in post-2000s Singapore. As part of the project, I interview artists, activists, and administrators whose practices involve themes or elements relating to social justice or change. I tell them that transcripts of our three- or four-hour interviews will be exhibited as part of the project's final showcase, but that, as part of the process, interviewees will have a chance before the show opens to redact anything they do not want made public.

I learned as much from the wealth of information they so generously shared with me as I did from what they chose to redact. The transcripts were exhibited with the redacted text covered in black boxes.

There were so many black boxes.

So many people in creative professions have left Singapore and are thriving, are making work I am pretty sure would be considered "out of bounds" in Singapore. When I let Elisha know what had happened, we both came to the conclusion that instead of expending time and energy on fighting what we knew was a lost cause, we'd cut the video from the show and leave the table upon which it was supposed to be shown empty in the center of the gallery. In addition, I wrote on it with correction fluid, a favorite medium for many a child who has vandalized a school table, to make sure that visitors knew it was not an artwork, so I would not get into trouble for exhibiting an object that was not approved as part of our license:

This is not a piece of art. This is the desk upon which Elisha Lim's film "Ruby" was going to be screened via a portable DVD player.

We apologise for being unable to screen it. The film has been rated NC-16 by the MDA and all films rated NC-16 or above require a security deposit of $10,000 from the venue/organiser in order to be screened.

The 52-second animation contains no sex, no nudity, no elements of horror, no violence, no drug references, no "foul" language and was submitted to a film festival in New York under the children's category.

It is available for free on YouTube.

Ironically, I think more people ended up watching the film because it was pulled.

———•———

████████ *Fear of Writing* █████ a writer struggling ██████
anxiety ██████████ scrutiny, ████████████████████
██████████████████████ politics, boundaries, bureaucracy and
censorship ████████████████████████████████████final
act.
████ ██
                                                                                    offi-
cial ████████ officers ████████████████
████████████████ stop them.
(allegedly unlicensed) ████████████ seize ██████ equipment.
████████████ distracting ████████████████████
██
████████████ planted ████████████████████████
████████████████████████ censor ████████████ seize █
██
████████ without warrant ████ Films Act. ████████████
implicated ████████████████████████████████
████████████████ Public Order Act ████████████ enforcement
████████████████████████████████ up to a year.

██████████████████████████████ *in* ████████
████████████████████ legal █ bureaucratic jargon ████
████████████████ scare ███████████████████
████████████ take you down, ████████████ Defamation
Licensing ████████████ Act. ████ Act. ████
Acts innumerable. ████████ ████████████████████ without trial ████████████ Act.

There is so much more that I wanted to tell you ████████
████████ OB markers shift ████████████████
████████ terrified ██████ the state, ██████████
██████████████████████████████████
██████ no documented evidence ████████████ omitted from this
manuscript.

████████████████ *Thin Line* ████████████████
██████████████████████████ Forces. It focused on something
that transpired with Derek, a former housemate who was a full-time
commando in the Singapore Army.

██ effort ██████████████████████████████
████████████████████ induction exercises ████████
████████████████████████ compulsory █
████████████████ required to undertake.
████████████████

██
██
████████████████ required ████████████████
████████████ uncomfortable ████████████████
████████████ The camera ████████████████
██████████████████████████████ He is shiv-
ering.

██████████████████ is laughing █████████ he is laughing ████████████████████ is finding this entertaining. ██████████ I am disoriented with fear ██ this realization that ████████████

████████████████████████ shots ███████████ wide shot ██████████ close-ups █████ individuals. ████████ tired, ████████████████ cries ███████████████ particularly amusing.

The video ends ███████████████████████████ ████████ a variation of the same ████████████ voices:

I want to serve my country.

██ ████████████████████████████████ rage █████ satirical ████ ███████████████████████ political ████████ angry. ████ pure comedy, ████████ disclaimer ████████ required by law, ███████████████ classification. ████ █████████████████████████ classification █████████████ political film. █████████████████ vet ████████ implicit ███████████ some blacklist.

Their response: ██████████████████

████████████████████████████████████ political ████████ government attention █████████████████ I withdrew ████████████ disappointment ██████ ████████████████████████████████████ ████████ caution. ████████████████████████████ ██████████ ashamed ███████████ I have something to lose—this new and beautiful life.

██████████████████████████ someone who should recognise you, doesn't.

The truth is, I am terrified ████████████████████ ██████ I'm terrified ███████████████████████ ███████████████████████████ I'm terrified ███ ██ ██ ████ I'm terrified ██████ permit ████████████████ con- trol ███████████████ home-not-home ██ live with the mistake ████████████ consequences ██ I am afraid ██ I am ashamed ██████ afraid ████████████████████████████ fear.

██████████ I'm terrified ████████████████ fear ████████ ██████ all the things I want to say, ████████████████████

██████████████████████████████████ *Fear of Writing* █

████████████ complacency ████████████████████████ ██████████ no danger, no real change ████████████████ ██████████ hijacked as entertainment ████████ engine of change."

██ ████████████████████████████ government-funded ████████ government policy.

██████████ *Fear of Writing* ███████████████████████ ██ mes- sage? ████████████████████████████ boundaries? ███ making art ████████████████████████████████ criminal or co-opted?

Which is worse?

———•———

Prior to *Tango,* I think many queer writers assumed that the literary arts in Singapore occupied an unofficial gray area that felt less policed than artistic media with wider reach.

For example, television has been historically far more policed than poetry. The MDA once fined a cable TV operator S$10,000 for screening an advertisement that featured a lesbian kiss, saying, "This is in breach of the TV advertising guidelines, which disallows advertisements that condone homosexuality."

Conversely, the Singapore Writers Festival always includes queer writers who speak about their work on panels. And the National Arts Council funds literary projects by openly queer authors despite the vague and dubious disclaimer that always follows its funding guidelines—one that notes how the council "prioritises funding proposals which do not advocate for lifestyles seen as objectionable by the general public."

Because of Singapore's decision to pump funding into the literary arts, writers in Singapore have opportunities available to them that a lot of struggling writers elsewhere would envy. But when *Tango* happened, this privilege started to feel like complicity I had to acknowledge. Every time I received a government grant, some part of me died with my tacit acceptance of that clause. And even when government grants put food on my table, denying my participation in my own oppression meant denying my own agency. And maybe that's the real reason this whole thing felt like betrayal: it felt as though it broke what had been an unspoken agreement:

Give us some money in exchange for the cultural cred you receive from showcasing queer authors. Give us a platform and we promise to behave.

Amidst all the ongoing fallout, a rep from the National Library made a public statement saying that the library's understanding of family was consistent with that of the Ministry of Social and Family Development and the Ministry of Education: one man, one woman, children.

At first, I hesitated to drop out of the festival because, as a freelance worker, I needed the money. Within the community, everyone assured one another that whatever decision each of us made was valid and that anyone who needed that income should not go hungry. I had contemplated attending my panels and bringing up the issue, but I could no longer picture myself being able to do that without crying.

One thing that really warmed me about the whole saga was how allies organized alongside us. Two women—straight, Chinese, and married with children—who were clearly well versed in political optics, organized a read-in in the foyer of the library's central branch. The invitation on Facebook was incredibly cheery: *Let's get together and read books!*

They went through the process of applying for a license, pitched the event as a read-in, and crowds of children and parents sat outside the library reading *Tango Makes Three* and *The White Swan Express*, which the organizers made available.

Around the same time, an activist from the community modified the logo from Penguin Books to mirror the cover of *Tango* while maintaining the original style. And across the bubbles of all my social media, penguins became a symbol of resistance.

Probably in response to the bad publicity it was receiving internationally, the National Library Board decided to make a compromise. The books would not be pulped, but they would not be housed in the children's section either. Instead, they could only be accessed by adults, and only by request.

"Compromise" has been an existing theme in the fight for queer justice in Singapore. For decades queer people were told that the retention of 377a, the law criminalizing "sex between men," was purely symbolic and that the compromise was that it would never be enforced.

But is this a truly a mutual compromise? Being criminalized for being oneself in exchange for not going to prison?

When 377a was finally repealed in 2023, the compromise was that Singapore's constitution be amended to protect the current definition of marriage—a union between a man and a woman—from any future legal challenges.

Is *this* truly a mutual compromise?

For the people who rallied for the book to be pulped, life went on as it had before. But many queer people still lost yet another part of the country that once felt like home.

Where was the compromise there?

———————•———————

I think often of the penguin-person spotted so many times on Stomp. I think of the images Stomp published: them shopping at Geylang Serai, buying ice cream at 7-Eleven, eating *bak chor mee* at some unnamed hawker center. But I think most often of them leaning casually out from the corridor of Block 234, looking as though they were hanging up the Singaporean flag, wearing that iconic *kebaya*. I like to imagine them drifting down the corridor after the photograph was taken, mask still on, face underneath covered with sweat, gracefully turning the corner of the stairs and disappearing to some place unknown.

One place Stomp didn't manage to catch them was the read-in outside the library. In fact, I don't think there are any images documenting the fact that they were there.

Trust me, however, when I say that they were.

I still don't know why penguin-person chose to wear that iconic *kebaya*, though.

Perhaps it was just a funny juxtaposition of disparate elements. Or an attempt to subvert a national icon. Or commentary on the body policing both women and queer people face.

Perhaps "a great way to fly" came to mind when thinking of compromise—penguins being birds that were given wings but were never able to take to the sky.

Where Are You From?

A woman on television speaks. Says
there are too many dark men
on the streets, too much land
they seem to have taken on loan
too many bones in their bodies
waiting to explode.

—POOJA NANSI, "TOO MANY"

The first time I am asked this question upon arriving in Canada, the question is mutual. My partner and I are staying at an Airbnb while waiting for school housing to be ready. The question comes from an American woman visiting Canada with her boyfriend. They are staying in the same house we are, and we are having a conversation in the kitchen.

She is excited—maybe a little too excited—to learn that we are from Singapore. It is 2018, *Crazy Rich Asians* has just become a phenomenon in North America, and she is shocked that neither of us has watched it.

"But it's about *you guyssss!*" she keeps insisting, despite the fact that I keep telling her otherwise.

I don't know how to explain to her without starting a two-hour lecture on how race and racism operate in Singapore that I am neither crazy rich nor Chinese, or how every time I pass an ad for that film, fury bubbles up within me. I don't know how to explain in the space of the two remaining minutes my microwave meal will take to heat up that, while it is significant for Asian Americans that Hollywood produced an all-Asian film, locating it in Singapore and populating it solely with East Asian people reinforced a kind of marginalization experienced by Singapore's racialized minorities.

The same woman asks, thrice in that one conversation, why my partner and I don't have Singaporean accents, even after we tell her that there is no one Singaporean accent, just like there is no one American accent. I don't know how to explain to her that everyone from everywhere has an accent—that "neutral" accents are a fiction created by power structures.

But I am jet-lagged and disoriented, so I walk across the kitchen, pretending my meal is almost ready, and, feeling mildly guilty, leave her to my infinitely more patient partner.

———◆———

That first year in Vancouver, because the film was still hot, I found myself having to explain my aversion to *Crazy Rich Asians* repeatedly. Explaining it to White friends and acquaintances got frustrating. But explaining it to East Asian friends and acquaintances was complicated by an additional layer of discomfort. No one wants to explain to members of a community that has been historically and systemically oppressed in the country they live in that they are oppressors in another. I avoided the topic as much as possible.

I completely understand the importance of seeing oneself represented on the big screen and appreciate how liberating it was for East Asian Americans to be able to see that on such a grand scale. But setting a film in an imaginary Singapore where roughly 25 percent of the population is either nonexistent or subservient to its main characters is just another form of erasure and cultural imperialism. What Hollywood has done to Asian Americans for more than a century, *Crazy Rich Asians* did to us with that film.

As I was growing up, "racial harmony" was a recurring topic in our social studies classes, but no one ever really talked about what that meant apart from the fact that people were allowed to practice different forms of religion, and the fact that we weren't supposed to say or do anything that might ignite a race riot akin to those that occurred in 1964 between Chinese and Malay people in Singapore following the country's short-lived merger with Malaysia.

But as much as we were taught in classrooms about how to be "racially harmonious" with one another, what happened outside of class was markedly different.

My primary school memories are filled with young Chinese children, undoubtedly influenced by the adults in their lives, making fun of the Indian, Malay, and other brown kids they went to school with. Shaking one's head side to side "like an Indian" was a common pastime. Referring to Malay people, Singapore's Indigenous community, as lazy was another. Saying that curry eaten by Indian people looked "like shit" and mimicking what was perceived to be an Indian accent were also routine.

And I wish I could say that it was just the kids. Teachers often laughed because they were not able to pronounce the "long and confusing" names of Indian and Malay students. In fact, Indian people were often used as disciplinary warnings by parents of Chinese children: "You better behave wait *mangali* come and catch you!"—a threat suggesting that if you did not behave, an Indian man would come and snatch you up.

As Singaporeans, we were taught that "Western countries" were full of racism and that Singapore was not. Like many other things we were taught in class, these lessons did not really pan out in everyday life.

———•———

It will come as no surprise that the pandemic put a magnifying glass on existing racial and class divisions in Singapore. I was in Vancouver at the time, devastated over the violence being enacted upon anyone who was, or looked, Chinese. My East Asian friends in the region were hurting as hate crimes against East Asian individuals spiked; some of them were afraid every time they had to leave the house.

In the early days of the pandemic, Singapore was seen as an example of a positive, decisive nation, garnering praise for low infection rates despite its population density and close proximity to China. It was one of the first countries to ban travel from Wuhan, and then the whole of China, an enormous feat, considering the amount of daily business travel and tourism that exists between the two countries. When the local infection number hit 110, the government of Singapore extended the ban to travelers from other hard-hit countries, such as Italy, France, Spain, and Germany. Singapore was one of the first countries to administer temperature screenings at airports and implement aggressive contact tracing. It was one of the first places to encourage masking and one of the last places to drop mask mandates. Early on, authorities even employed "social distance ambassadors," individuals trained to gently remind people not to stand too close together in public settings. Strict laws concerning home isolation were designed for those with symptoms; people isolated with Covid would receive messages at random times of the day that required them to take photos of themselves in their apartments in order to verify their locations.

On March 12, 2020, Prime Minister Lee Hsien Loong declared during a public broadcast that what made Singapore different from other countries was that its citizens had confidence in one another.

We don't leave anyone behind.

When numbers started spiking across the globe, and flight routes started closing, Singapore started calling home citizens who were studying abroad. I felt immense pressure to leave Canada. The threat felt ominous and omnipotent, and every potential decision felt fraught with terrible possibilities. What if my partner got ill while I was away and I could not come back because of flight restrictions? What if I returned to Singapore straightaway and then could not get back to Canada because my study permit expired while I was away? What if being away interfered with my ability to apply for a work permit once I graduated?

I decided to stay in Canada and watch Singapore from afar through the window of my computer screen. It was like living two realities—the everyday in which you exist physically, and the other everyday in which you exist virtually, separated from loved ones by a sixteen-hour time difference and eighteen hours of travel.

Over the next few weeks, I watched friends broadcast their return to Singapore on social media. Everywhere on the island newly returned citizens posted photos and videos of their isolation experiences. Compared to what was happening in other countries, their #StayHomeNotice looked like a holiday. Singaporeans returning from high-risk countries and unable to isolate were housed for free in hotels for fourteen days upon arrival. One acquaintance practiced his flag-dancing skills in the confines of his room, broadcasting the joyful solo performance via Facebook. Another photographed himself lounging in an armchair, looking thoughtful. Many photos showed plastic food containers filled with pasta, croissants, fruit, and other varieties of food—meals that were provided by the hotels. I watched from far away, marveling at the variety of fancy interiors, comfortable-looking beds, high-rise views.

Returning home began to resemble a bizarre and surreal version of going on holiday. I was happy that people I knew were being taken care of.

———◆———

When the first few migrant construction workers got sick, it was early days. Singapore's overall numbers were still low, so no one paid attention. When three more workers tested positive, still no one paid attention. After all, the virus was not *only* attacking migrant workers—it was attacking everyone. The only people who rang the alarm were activists familiar with the living conditions in which many migrant construction workers in Singapore lived.

Very broadly speaking, when Singaporeans speak of "migrant workers," they are referring to workers who come from other Asian countries, working low-wage jobs when they arrive. These workers pay high fees to recruitment agencies in search of work placements. They are men from India and Bangladesh who become the laborers who build the roads, public housing, and tourist landmarks that Singapore is so well known for. Women from the Philippines and Indonesia who leave their families back home to take care of other people's families and their households. Workers are charged thousands of dollars in agency costs, sometimes selling land or taking out loans to afford them. Being in debt ends up leaving them vulnerable to the unbalanced power dynamics that already exist and that such high debt reinforces. Voicing concerns about squalid living conditions, overwork, abuse, or nonpayment might mean losing your job and being sent home with less money than you came with.

Some "maid agencies"—employment agencies responsible for helping families hire migrant domestic workers—have been known to have their workers on "display" in their storefronts, simulating housework. They tend to dolls as though they are real babies. They iron clothes and fold laundry. Some are made to sit beneath signs that identify them as "budget maids," suggesting they can be "purchased" at a good rate. One agency tagged women by race and country of origin: Filipinos were "smarter," Indonesians "less bright," and Burmese "sweet natured and compliant."

Because domestic workers are expected to live with their employers, cases of physical, verbal, and sexual abuse can go unreported and unnoticed for long periods of time. Many domestic workers are made to live in tiny rooms originally designed for storage, and employers are only obligated to provide them with one day of rest per month—a rule the government finally made mandatory in January 2023. I can only imagine how the pandemic, specifically the periods during which people had to isolate at home, affected domestic workers already living in abusive situations.

While migrant domestic workers are hired by families, migrant construction workers are employed by companies and are ferried back and forth in the cargo beds of open trucks between worksites and dorms, where they often lived in cramped conditions. As the pandemic progressed and the number of workers falling ill increased, photos taken inside some of these dorms started circulating on social media, and the conditions that had been highlighted by activists for years became a focus of attention and concern.

For many workers, small dorm rooms that house anywhere between six and twenty men are hotbeds for any sort of virus. In the initial stages of the outbreak, Professor Mohan Dutta from Massey University interviewed forty-five migrant workers. He learned that some workers did not even have access to soap and adequate cleaning supplies. And that in some cases, one hundred men were sharing five toilets and five showers.

In any society, the poorest among us are often the most vulnerable, and in Singapore, the discrimination against and abuse of migrant workers seem to emerge from an intersection of racism, classism, and xenophobia.

Rich and often White professionals who migrate to Singapore to work in corporate jobs are often referred to as "foreign talent"—shorthand that differentiates them from migrant workers, who are colloquially referred to as "foreign workers." And just like in other countries, migrant labor is often blamed for job scarcity and dense urban living. One phenomenon I find particularly strange is Singaporeans' attitudes to migrant workers with whom they share similar ethnic backgrounds. From my experience, rather than attempting to build solidarity across class, Indian and Chinese Singaporeans are often quick to differentiate themselves from their "foreign" counterparts with the refrain "We are not like them."

When news about the virus spreading in migrant workers' dorms went mainstream, comment threads became unbearable to read. While the news garnered outrage from some quarters on behalf of the workers, it also garnered a second kind of outrage—one that blamed the workers' alleged lack of hygiene for the spread of the virus. The stereotype of Indian people being "dirty" was one I'd heard since childhood. And as more and more migrant workers from South Asia began to come to Singapore, they seemed to bear double the brunt of this stereotype.

I wish I could say that racist attitudes towards migrant workers were limited to a small pocket of the community with no real power over the fates of racialized people. Unfortunately, this is not the case.

For example, former Member of Parliament Choo Wee Khiang will go down in history for talking about his experience of driving to Little India, an area patronized largely by migrant workers and Singaporeans of Indian descent, and how it was "pitch dark, not because there was no light, but because there were too many Indians around." Around the same time Donald Trump was trumpeting his ideas about building a wall along the U.S.-Mexico border, Denise Phua, another Singapore Parliament member, suggested building fences around communal areas such as playgrounds and void decks (open spaces in housing blocks) in Little India to keep "congregations" of migrant workers—which she referred to as "walking time-bombs"—away from the rest of the community.

For days after hearing this, all I could think about was the word "communal" and what it was supposed to mean if it did not include all members of a community.

My earliest memory of experiencing racism involved a kindergarten classmate referring to me as "Blackie" and telling me I could not play with him and his friends. In my teens, I remember looking for part-time jobs whilst in school and realizing how many professional possibilities were closed to me by the phrases "Chinese preferred" and "Must speak Mandarin." I've been excluded from conversations by my

Chinese classmates and colleagues and have been hung up on by real estate agents whose first question upon hearing my housing query was almost always "What race are you?" and whose goodbyes were almost always "Sorry, Chinese only."

But even so, I've not had it as bad as others. Being mixed-race and racially ambiguous, I am read differently depending on who is in the room. And being on the lighter side of brown has often shielded me from more severe racism and colorism targeted at Malay and Indian people, as well as anyone with skin darker than mine.

When I was growing up, being light-skinned was considered, along with being thin, the epitome of beauty. I rarely saw advertisements of anyone that looked like me. The people sitting down to family dinners on posters promoting soon-to-be-built condos were always Chinese, with the occasional White father and mixed, light-skinned child thrown in for variety. Beauty products that promised "fairer," more beautiful skin "in just x number of days" were common—lightening creams, lightening deodorants, lightening cleansers, lightening scrubs. And while I am not really interested in being some company's target market, I do know that the media that surround us reinforces existing attitudes, and that the hegemony of what is considered acceptable, preferable, and desirable trickles back down into the everyday.

When I say that I am read differently depending on who is in the room, what I mean is that I experience racism differently depending on what assumptions are made about me by whomever I happen to be sharing space with at the time. In Singapore, my "in-between" shade meant that while I was often a target of racism, more often I was witness to it secondhand because the people being racist thought I was in on the joke.

For example, I remember a classmate signing my high school autograph book when we were thirteen. My little green book was filled with cute rhymes, jokes, I-loves-yous, and refrains of the ever-eternal, cringe-inducing "Stay cool and funky" when I passed it to Meiling. She took it back to her desk and giggled the whole time as she put in her message and passed the book back to me with great enthusiasm:

God made the day
God made the night.
God made Indians
and forgot to paint them white!

Hahaha. See you next year!

Meiling.

At first, I was too shocked to react. The shock morphed into confusion. She did not seem to have passed me the book with any malice—did this mean she thought I would find her words funny? My best friend, also in our class, had dark skin and an Indian surname. In fact, our class was one of two first-year classes that included Malay and Indian students, which means that she was in the company of Indian classmates every day. By the time I had processed the note and was able to get angry, Meiling was gone, and all I could do was tear the page out of my book.

I am ashamed to say this became a pattern for me—this shock and confusion, followed by anger that came too late—and I never ended up saying anything. Not when the incident with the autograph book happened. Not when my junior college classmate told me that my face "looked *okay* for a mixed person." Not when another classmate told me they would "never date anyone from Africa" because they were "too dark."

It was only in my early twenties that I started voicing objection. To the colleague who said there was no point installing a CCTV camera out-side our office because the area was populated by Indian workers and they all looked the same anyway. To a fellow lecturer who worked at the college where I taught and said that having too many Indian students in one class is never good because they talk too much. To the other lecturer, who said it was hard explaining some topics to the Malay women who wear *tudungs* because of how closed-minded they were.

I don't remember which last straw turned me into the quintessential "Angry Brown Woman." I just know it was such a long time coming, that once I started, I could not stop.

◆

In my opinion, the policies put in place to ensure racial harmony in Singapore are sometimes the very mechanisms that hinder conversations about race and maintain the status quo. As well intentioned as they may be, they do not take into account frameworks of power and sometimes perpetuate discrimination instead of punishing it.

For example, one's ability to buy or sell public housing (which houses roughly 80 percent of the population) can depend on one's race. Every area in Singapore has an "ethnic quota"—a system meant to foster racial integration in housing estates. The scheme aims to ensure that the proportion of residents in any given area matches the wider demographics of Singapore's racial makeup. The makeup is defined by a framework called "CMIO"—"Chinese Malay Indian Others."

This means that if you are not Chinese, you are often only allowed to sell your flat to another non-Chinese person, thus cutting out a large majority of potential buyers and making your flat harder to sell. Tangentially, this has also resulted in racially charged language concerning the buying and selling of property, with real estate agents often asking people who inquire about properties what "race" they are. Unfortunately, this is a culture that has trickled down into the business of renting and leasing property as well. When my partner and I went to view a rental apartment, the agent told us we were lucky: the only other family who was interested in the place was Indian and the owner preferred not to rent to them.

My partner and I exchanged silent glances that affirmed we were not going to take the apartment, I alerted the agent to the fact that I was, in part, Indian, and we walked.

Then there is the Sedition Act, a law designed to criminalize, among other things, "the promotion of feelings of ill-will and hostility between different races." Again, because the law does not take into account frameworks of power, it sometimes backfires, punishing angry reactions to racism rather than racism itself.

For instance, when Nets released a nationwide advertisement for one of its new electronic payment systems, it featured a Chinese actor in brownface pretending to be Indian. Neither the actor nor the media company who created it were taken to task.

However, siblings Preetipls and Subhas, two young Indian artists who made a satirical music video chastising the people who had created the ad, were called up by the police. According to Preetipls, they were at the police station for nine hours that day, and she had her laptop, phone, and hard disc confiscated.

"Like I killed someone," she mused in an interview.

In my opinion, incidents like this make people afraid to speak about race, turn minorities into scapegoats, and end up perpetuating the problem. The irony is that suppressing conversation about race, even if unintentional, is impossible given how race-obsessed we were made to be while growing up. Every other form I had to fill in as a teenager included the boxes "Chinese," "Malay," "Indian," or "Other" right after our names—"Other," a word I ended up associating with myself for years. On our National IDs, our race comes directly after our name. In "One People, One Nation," a National Day song we sang every year, we chorused on about how "every creed and every race, has its role and has its place." Differentiating ourselves and each other by race is so automatic in Singapore that if you cannot immediately be placed into a recognizable category, it is perfectly common for someone to just ask, "What are you?"

What is your role? What is your place?

During my most recent trip back to Singapore, a taxi driver, while staring at me in the rearview mirror, asked where I was from—a question I have gotten countless times in the country I was born in and spent almost four decades living in. When I said I was Singaporean, he looked confused and asked what I was. By the time I was a teenager, I learned never to bother responding with what my ID card says—that I am Eurasian—because that only leads to more questions. I've learned never to respond by listing my actual heritage—Indian, Sri Lankan, Japanese, Irish, Portuguese, English—because that ends up confirming the asker's belief that I am not from Singapore.

Instead, I just tell them I am mixed and pop in my headphones. Because I've learned not to talk about race.

————◆————

So here's the thing: I don't necessarily want to see myself reflected in *Crazy Rich Asians*. I don't want to see myself throwing unnecessarily lavish parties or languishing amidst glitzy architecture built by exploited migrant workers. I don't want to see myself as a player in some story in which Singapore is just spectacle and prop. I don't want to see myself in a film that essentially celebrates the very phenomena which disenfranchise so many poor people in Singapore.

Had *Crazy Rich Asians* been a story set in the United States, it might have been closer to the "Asian *Black Panther*" many deemed it to be. But so long as it exists in a version of Singapore where Brown people live solely for comic relief or to open car doors for Constance Wu, a version of Singapore that makes this highly multiracial city look as though it is populated solely by Chinese people, all it does is reinforce existing power structures and perpetuate the invisibility and marginalization that racialized people in Singapore face every day—another dose of the same, just backed up by Hollywood this time.

What I do want is for Chinese and other East Asian Americans who very understandably crave representation in the media to remember that the catharsis this movie provides them is still rooted in the imperialist power that Hollywood wields when it comes to its representations of other countries and cultures outside of North America. What I want is for this film to exist as a tiny drop of water in a giant international pool of cultural output that provides a counterpoint to capitalist, consumerist frivolity and to U.S.-centric understandings of race and place.

What I want is media that does not leave anyone behind.

———————•———————

Among all the photos concerning migrant workers on social media during the pandemic, one stood out. It was an image of the small field that sits across the street from an apartment I used to stay in. Migrant workers used to hang out there every Sunday—their one day off per week. I loved the joyful energy they brought to the neighborhood during the weekend.

The photo showed the park completely empty and was taken by the member of parliament in charge of our neighborhood. He wrote about how migrant workers used to "congregate" there, "inconveniencing" residents.

He said: "It takes a virus to empty out the space."

In mid-April 2020, Prime Minister Lee Hsien Loong took to the podium once more to address the nation regarding the pandemic:

"To our migrant workers, let me emphasize again: we will care for you, just like we care for Singaporeans."

In the early days of the pandemic, thousands of workers were isolated within their crowded dorms to stem the spread of Covid. One headline in *The Guardian* quoted a worker: "We're in a prison." According to a post from the migrant worker advocacy group Transient Workers Count 2, in one particular dorm, a manager placed twenty workers in a shared room with no toilet, and with a door that locked from the outside, for over a day. The workers had been deemed close contacts of another worker who had tested positive for Covid and the manager did not want them to move around the facility while management prepared a room for them.

By mid-June 2020, almost 98 percent of people who tested positive for Covid-19 in Singapore were migrant workers living in dorms. We know this because of the new way the media started to present the stats—dividing the migrant workers from the rest of us. In a graph presented by Channel NewsAsia, they are referred to as "dorm residents" and "work permit holders," while Singaporeans and permanent residents are referred to as "community."

The graph, in its simplicity, seemed to describe perfectly what the pandemic had uncovered:

There is community.

And then there are those who reside outside of it.

In September 2021, the BBC reported that even though life in Singapore was returning to normal, many migrant workers were experiencing "one of the longest periods of Covid confinement faced by anyone anywhere in the world." Close to 300,000 workers were banned from mixing with the general public until a handful of workers were allowed to go out under a "pilot scheme"—the first day of which saw fifty dormitory workers given permission to spend four hours outside of their dormitories unsupervised. Those not selected had to be content with views of the city while traveling, mostly in lorries, between their dormitory and worksite.

In June 2022, the *Financial Times* reported that while Singapore had lifted almost all its remaining Covid measures, a maximum of only 25,000 of the 280,000 workers who lived in dormitories were allowed to travel on weekdays beyond their dormitories, their worksites, and the eight recreation centers built for them—and only on the condition that their trips be limited to eight hours and that they tell authorities where they were going. Fifty thousand workers were allowed to travel on weekends.

In 2020, amidst the cacophony of people speaking about the spread of Covid-19 among migrant worker communities, there were only a handful of spaces where one could find migrant workers speaking for themselves. One of them was Artists On Permits ft Singapore, a Facebook group dedicated to writings by migrant workers in Singapore.

Alongside writing from men who spoke about missing their families, about being confined, about their fears of getting ill, there was writing that expressed admiration for Singapore, its beauty. But more surprising to me was all the poetry that expressed deep attachment to and deep love for Singapore, with one writer describing how Singapore lives in his heart.

Still today, I am struck by how, even in such dark times, these men are willing to offer us beauty, even when all we have is ugliness to offer in return.

Thin Line

The day I understand fully that Singapore is no longer my home, and perhaps never was, I am sitting in my dorm, scrolling through Facebook. I stop short when I come across a news article about a former student of mine. There's a photo at the top of the article. He smiles for the camera. He holds an ice-cream cone in one hand, pets his dog with the other. They must have used an old photo because it's been ten years since we shared a classroom and this is exactly how I remember him—young, spirited, his whole life ahead of him.

He has been arrested for supplying drugs to friends. The article says he will serve twenty years. During his time in prison, he will receive twenty-four strokes of the cane—it says he will be tied naked to a flogging post and whipped by a man trained to exert as much strength as possible. The four-foot-long cane will measure up to half an inch in diameter. Inmates do not know when their caning will be carried out—they find out the day it happens. The man who wields the cane practices on dummies and sandbags. By the time my student is free, he will be forty-nine years old.

The title of the article is pure clickbait. It quotes him:

I'm scared, it says. *The skin normally tears after three strokes.*

For a good minute, I am sure this is a prank. That if I scroll down long enough, the internet will grant both him and me mercy with some sort of distasteful April Fools' reveal.

But the scrolling plunges me into the comments section, and the content there is worse than the article. In a morbid combination of grief, rage, and disbelief, I find myself reading comment after comment, trying to wrap my head around the self-righteous glee I find:

Give it to him, one person says.

Serves him right, says another.

A more measured comment notes that he is lucky: he is rich and from London—had he been yet another poor brown boy from Malaysia, he would have gotten the death penalty.

I don't sleep that night.

———————•———————

The word "caning," when used to refer to corporal punishment, often feels less severe to Singaporeans than it actually is. Because as children we were so used to what our parents did to us with the thin, two-dollar *rotan* they bought from provision stores, we grew up believing that getting hit was a natural consequence of a failed test or rude remark. Some of what my classmates experienced—being whipped with a belt for failing a test, for example—also made my mother's application of the *rotan* seem less serious to me. If a *rotan* was unavailable at the time of punishment, getting smacked across the face would do.

A *good tight slap* was not an exception; it was a rule. It was not something our parents defended as appropriate—it was an act so ordinary that they never had to.

For years, I believed in that *good tight slap.* I wished it upon children crying in restaurants, at bus stops, in malls. A *good tight slap* was how they would learn. A *good tight slap* was how *we* learned.

Every time the thought surfaced, I would push it away, scold myself. But in the face of every screaming child, there it was again, like a reflex, this ugly voice not my own but also, all my own.

Every now and then, I revisit articles about my student's imprisonment and punishment and consider my complicity in violence.

One day, I type his name into Facebook to see what people are sharing. An acquaintance calls him stupid. Says the punishment is just. Even as I unfriend her, her profile picture haunts me—her family-friendly avatar of two fresh-faced parents, their young son between them, his future still a blank slate.

———◆———

I don't tell people this, but I often fantasize about Singapore being overrun by zombies. Imagine that: this tiny city with no natural resources, no high ground, nowhere to run except to sea.

I imagine those living in close quarters would turn first: migrant workers forced into inhumane conditions would pour from their dorms, tearing down the very city they built. Primary school kids sitting forty to a class would not know enough to run when a classmate went rabid. Bunkers and bunkers of national servicemen would shuffle amok in camouflage, feasting on the people they were supposed to protect.

The destruction would be quick. The country's small size, the very quality that made it so easily controllable, would instead become the seed of its downfall.

———◆———

The first time I understand the extent of horde mentality, I learn that some friends are under police questioning for being part of a silent protest. The protest comprises seven people standing in a row in a train carriage, holding copies of *1987*, a collection of accounts written by alleged "Marxist Conspirators" detained without trial under the Internal Security Act. All seven participants wear blindfolds but hold the books open in front of their faces as though they are reading them. The photos circulate online like wildfire.

When I ask one friend how the police identified them, she tells me that they didn't. People online had decided the seven were troublemakers and trawled the internet, piecing identities together by matching facial features, hair, and stature to tagged images taken at political gatherings.

How do you avoid the police when the police are everyone?

———•———

The first time I learned the word "fail," I was four years old and obsessed with drawing cyclones. My mother had rented *The Wizard of Oz* and now cyclones were everywhere: in blue marker on the home whiteboard, in pencil on my bedroom floor, in gray crayon on all the pages of my drawing pad.

I think I was obsessed with cyclones because they were the first things I realized I could draw "correctly." All you needed to do was draw continuous loops from the top of your paper, making them smaller and smaller till they reached a pinpoint at the bottom. I enjoyed drawing people and animals, but they never really looked like real people or animals. To my child-mind, my cyclones always looked like cyclones.

In kindergarten one day, we were tasked to draw faces. Our teacher piled a bag of colorful plastic masks on the table for us to copy and set out the crayons. I said I wanted to draw a cyclone. She told me I'd "better not"—that if I did, I would "fail."

This is my earliest memory of school.

———•———

We don't get tornadoes or cyclones in Singapore. We're too far from fault lines for earthquakes. We are bolstered by countries that bear the brunt of tsunamis, and for the most part, our flash floods wreck property but are never severe enough to kill people. In this way, we are lucky.

In some other countries, an undead apocalypse is used as a metaphor to chart out game plans for natural disasters. According to a Defense Department document obtained by CNN, the U.S. military used a planet-wide attack by the walking dead as a training template for planning for large-scale emergencies. In 2015, British medical journal *The Lancet* jokingly published a paper that looked at the epidemiology, treatment, and prevention of an undead virus. The United States's Centers for Disease Control and Prevention has equated being prepared for an undead apocalypse to being prepared for real-life disaster.

A recent academic document concerning the undead came out in the University of Leicester's *Journal of Physics Special Topics*. According to the research, based on the assumption that a bite from the undead would cause immediate infection, an apocalypse would decimate humanity in less than a year—in fact, findings suggest that the population would drop to under two hundred people in just over three months.

When taking into account geographical isolation, human reproduction, and the ability of humans to fight back, it was found that the population would still drop into the hundreds, but that the last of the undead would be killed off about three years into the pandemic.

I can't find any information that takes into account, though, one very basic characteristic of viruses—their ability to adapt.

What happens when a corpse learns to open a door, to climb stairs, to organize? What happens when its actions resemble more and more those of your father, your mother, your neighbors, your friends?

———————————— • ————————————

Every day, I wait for the ugly inside me to surface, for the monster to reveal its horrific face. I look into the mirror and think about my ugly heart. Skin ashen, jaw unhinged, my body as dead on the outside as I am on the inside. I imagine the worms under my tongue, rotting my speech. The spiders in my chest, waiting for flies. They string webs across my ribs. They have me outnumbered. I can hear them spinning. This is the embodiment of apathy. A corpse cannot care. I want to stop caring.

———•———

In the midseason finale of *The Walking Dead*'s Season 6, Deanna is bitten by one of the infected—it is only a matter of time before she becomes one of them.

The horde is approaching and she decides she wants to stay behind. The other survivors part with her and go a single different way, in search of a new home. They leave her a loaded gun.

In the final montage, Deanna lays in her bed, gun to the underside of her jaw, bent on killing herself before she turns. She hears the infected making their way to her room, their slow shuffle, their lifeless moans. She gets out of bed, a fever-dream of fury. She stumbles to the door and turns the gun on them instead.

When she runs out of bullets, the camera zooms in on her face and she lets out a primal scream. We're not sure, though, because the sequence is masked by soundtrack. She is pale from the virus. Ragged, weak. Her eyes bulge, almost inhuman, her mouth is open so wide, her lower jaw seems to come loose. This is the final shot we see of her.

Viewers still argue over whether that moment was a scream of rage or the point at which she herself became undead; so much tension surrounding this thin line between human and monster, so slight we can't tell the difference.

———•———

Dr. Steven Schlozman of Harvard Medical School suggests that if an undead apocalypse were to occur, it would likely stem from a mutated virus passed from an animal to a human.

I hope he is wrong. That when we are gone, the animals will thrive. I hope our hunger will be specific, and will spare them. I hope those who run the farms and zoos will see what's coming—that they will unlock every gate, turn the fence off on every enclosure.

Let the pacing lions have their day—let them sprint their way to our forests, let their cubs prance across our parks. Let the elephants lumber alongside empty vehicles lining Orchard Road. Let Ah Meng's grandchildren, released from servitude, bound towards our reserves. May their families never be imprisoned again.

Let us perform this final act of kindness.

———◆———

What does cruelty look like?

According to information from *Prison Insider*, Singapore's incarcerated sleep on straw mats in the windowless cells they are confined to twenty-two hours a day. There is no fan to provide relief from the sweltering heat, and the interior lighting is never switched off. The only way to tell night from day is through the small holes in the prison wall. Because all prison activity is conducted indoors, this may be the only sunlight an inmate sees for years. Family photos are allowed with special permission. Inmates are allowed to write two letters per month and are allowed one thirty-minute, face-to-face visit a month.

I imagine my student sitting in his cell, which he probably shares with three other men. I imagine him as the bright teenager I once knew.

If the apocalypse comes, our incarcerated might be the only people who do not turn into monsters—the iron bars intended to protect us from them inevitably protecting them from us.

———◆———

After the end comes another end, and this is how I imagine it:

The last of the infected starves to death, its groans becoming one with the soil. The wind ruptures through rows and rows of uninhabited flats. Malls glisten under tropical sun, mannequins are doomed to wear one single outfit till the end of time. Driverless car after driverless car bottleneck the expressway, en route to the airport, completely still. Emptiness and excess lose both their meanings and become one and the same.

I never imagine the spaces I've actually existed in—old schools, former workplaces, husks of so many temporary homes.

No, I always return to the glistening landscape of tourist brochures, this view from outside so much less painful: shiny buildings scraping empty sky, the perpetual collapsing of waves, mechanical trees, their robot branches reaching for the clouds.

Watch the island undo itself. Watch the trees grow wild.

How beautiful you look, my once-homeland, now that you are free.

Dinner on Monster Island

You've handled me with scare
and I've responded with fear
and that is exactly
how you wanted it to be.

—MICHAELA THERESE, "HANDLE WITH SCARE"

Monster Island is always the same. You get plonked in the middle of a little island armed with a trusty water gun, primed to shoot any meanies that come your way. Masked slashers, chain saws in hand. Crafty vampires primed for a feast. Werewolves waiting for the fattening of the moon. Zombie hordes hungry for brains.

Dinner on Monster Island is Level 15 of *Zombies Ate My Neighbors*—a run-and-gun video game Sega released when I was a tween, which I discovered in my thirties, and which I still haven't quite gotten the hang of. It is also my go-to way of describing the country in which I lived for thirty-seven years. It's got a ring to it that I enjoy, and "Monster Island" sounds like it could be the name of a horror theme park I might love to visit one day.

Around the same time the game was released, I was learning a lot about the island on which I was born. My mother, adamant, taught me that Singapore was the safest place in the world to live. My grandmother, cautious, taught me that I should never say anything bad about the government. A secondary school art teacher taught me that Singapore could be viewed as somewhat of a theme park—specifically, "Disneyland with the Death Penalty," a phrase coined by Canadian American writer William Gibson. In 1993, he had written an article characterizing Singapore as bland, conformist, consumerist, and authoritarian. I did not get to read it till I was in college because in an act of what seemed like ironic agreement with some of Gibson's opinions, the government banned the entire magazine in which the article was published. When I finally got my hands on it as part of a college module on Art Business, I found that the long-form piece rang problematic on several levels. While Gibson does get a handful of things right, his tone makes him come across as a tourist who, in seeking out some "exotic" "Asian" adventure, accidentally landed himself in a place where everything is disappointingly clean and, even more boringly, works.

It felt kind of strange to me that the government wanted to keep it from the public—if anything, surely an article like this, when combined with a good dose of postcolonial resentment, might have stoked nationalism rather than dissent. But then again, even though the article felt somewhat one-dimensional, the title resonated, and continues to resonate, with me.

Disneyland with the Death Penalty.

As a kid, I thought the death penalty was reserved for murderers. I learned about it primarily from American television—legal shows my mother was fond of before she got born again and started believing in more spiritual forms of justice. To me, the death penalty was a horrible thing that happened far away. That people were hanged in my own home country came as a shock.

Almost three decades later, the death penalty remains alive and well in Singapore; the government believes it acts as a deterrent against serious crimes like murder and drug trafficking. Not even pandemic-induced social distancing managed to mitigate its stronghold, with 2020 marking the first time a man was sentenced to death in Singapore via Zoom—the second time this had happened worldwide.

While I find the prevailing use of the death penalty disturbing, I find the public's attitude towards it almost more so. Responses to the execution of drug couriers—many of whom are poor—are particularly troubling, with the general public appearing to have no issue with the state killing people who seem largely disenfranchised and desperate to make a living.

Furthermore, to my knowledge, there is no evidence that the elimination of these middlemen has had any impact on the people who hire them.

What I find most disturbing is this lack of empathy, which sometimes manifests in gleeful support of archaic punishment but, more often than not, exhibits as an apathetic shrug: *He knew the law.* Outside of social justice circles, there is little to no conversation about whether the law is just: what matters is that *he knew the law.* After all, the law exists for all our collective benefit. If those who break it are not punished, what, then, of our collective safety?

But who does this collective safety belong to and what does it look like? It feels impossible to me, in this day and age of widening wage gaps, that people who fear for our collective safety do not also fear the possibility that someone they love might one day live through circumstances so financially dire that they too might end up on death row. Surely the choice between feeding one's family and letting them starve, even if the former involves risky behavior, is not so hard to understand or empathize with? Surely anyone living through late-stage capitalism understands how we are all vulnerable to precarity?

Surely even if you believe that killing someone is an expression of justice, you understand that someday you, or someone you love, might need mercy?

———————— • ————————

The years leading up to my departure from Singapore and immediately following it felt increasingly merciless. The slow creep of government overreach seemed to have settled quietly on everyone's skin.

For activists, news about the Protection from Online Falsehoods and Manipulation Bill (POFMA), which granted the government power to decide what constitutes a falsehood, and the power to punish said falsehood, was cause for alarm. It felt very much like a follow-up to measures taken under the Online News Licensing Scheme (ONLS), implemented in 2013. This scheme requires local websites that post at least one article a week about current affairs in Singapore over a period of two months, and that have 50,000 or more visitors a month, to apply for a government license and to deposit a performance bond of $50,000. Under this license, they must comply with any orders from regulators to take down content that is deemed objectionable. Prior to the passing of the bill, Minister of Information Yaacob Ibrahim told the BBC that it was important for Singaporeans to "read the right thing."

The internet, a space that changed the face of activist organizing and civil society engagement in Singapore, enabling yearly in-person events such as Pink Dot—an annual public picnic in which people turn up in support of Singapore's queer community—to grow, and one-off phenomena such as the AWARE extraordinary general meeting of 2009 to transpire, was slowly becoming "regulated" in ways that were disturbing.

Shortly after the Protection from Online Falsehoods and Manipulation Bill came the Foreign Interference (Countermeasures) Act of 2021, which Reporters Without Borders described as a "legal monstrosity with totalitarian leanings." Seeking to "protect the public interest by counteracting acts of foreign interference," the 249-page bill was passed into law after just three weeks. However, as journalist Kirsten Han pointed out, the bill's terms were so broadly defined that "foreign principal" included "foreigner" under its umbrella, with "foreigner" being further defined to include "any individual who isn't a citizen of Singapore," essentially catching permanent residents in its net. According to Han, the bill defines "engaging in conduct on behalf of foreign principal" so widely that it captures a lot of legitimate activity undertaken by civil society organizations, arts groups, associations, and activists. To make matters worse, she notes that while a lot of the legislation targets "politically significant persons," such as members of parliament, "the relevant authority can designate you as a 'politically significant person' as long as your activities are directed 'towards a political end in Singapore.'"

But despite what looked like dystopia landing on one's doorstep, there was no real resistance to the implementation of these bills apart from a small minority of vocal activists and concerned citizens. For many, nothing seems to have changed; the rule of law is a weighted blanket guaranteeing peace, order, and stability for the majority of the country.

And if I were to be completely honest with myself, it was not the government that disappointed me—you cannot be disappointed by something you don't believe in. What disappointed me was the people. The fact that all the things I consider deplorable and alarming—the overreach, the censorship, the homophobia, the violent and draconian punishments—seemed so permissible for so many of my fellow Singaporeans, who kept voting in the same government again and again. And the fact that this made me feel so alone. I realized that every time someone I knew got "into trouble," the state was not only in the arm of the law, but in the voice of its people.

When artist Seelan Palay was arrested, unarmed, by six police officers for "staging an unlawful performance without a permit," I saw the state in one of my fellow adjuncts: he laughed while reading the news off his phone during lunch, saying that his former student had asked for it.

When historian PJ Thum argued for what he saw as a lack of evidence justifying the use of detention in relation to Operation Coldstore, and was grilled for six hours by a government committee, I saw the state in the people who flooded online comment threads, turning the event into a spectator sport, questioning his credentials and integrity.

Questions we do not ask enough: What is the role of citizen complicity in government oppression? How do fear and disempowerment drive us to police one another? If we feed our neighbors to the monster at lunchtime, will it return for us at dinner?

A couple of years before I left, a family member, often vocal about gender issues online, was doxed by an angry stranger. They found a photo of her attending a queer gathering, looked up her professional history, and circulated her details and work address on a local online hate group. The photo was one I had posted.

We were both terrified, and it was my fault. I untagged every photo of her I'd ever posted on social media. I scrolled through years of images and status updates that placed us together at political events and made sure they were not linked back to her. It felt like I had put her in danger and that I should have known better. Instead of blaming a culture of homophobia, misogyny, and snitching, I blamed myself. It did not matter what I understood to be true—that the perpetrator was the doxer, and not me. Because even if you do not fear for yourself, you will fear for the ones you love.

I found myself operating on a whole new level of self-surveillance, and for the first time in years, I thought twice before posting political opinions online. I scanned my friends list for people I did not know well, and attempted divination. A man cuddles his dog—how does he vote? A woman holds a birthday cake—is she homophobic? An old schoolmate makes a peace sign at the camera—would they tell on me if they recognized my face in a crowd of protesters?

If they showed no signs of solidarity, I deleted them from my list— something I would have never done a few months prior, given how essential social media visibility is to freelancers working in the arts in Singapore. In some impossible estimation of cost-benefit analysis, I decided that these connections were no longer worth the risk. My behavior somehow felt both paranoid and justified. There seemed to be only two spheres one could operate in: fear or malice. I guess a third sphere—one so many of my friends still operate in—was courage.

But after so many years of caring and fearing, watching members of my extended community get into trouble, courage no longer seemed worth the consequence.

Even now, miles away, a hard ball of anxiety sits in my stomach as I approach the end of this manuscript.

What unseen consequences will be unleashed with this book once it becomes its own entity out in the world and comes under scrutiny? Who will it inevitably harm?

———◆———

You can take the girl out of the country, but you can't take the country out of the girl. It's an absolute cliché but turned out to be true for me.

When I first got to Canada, I moved into school housing—a tiny studio apartment in a building filled with international students and Canadian students from outside of Vancouver. It took me a while to settle into my new life in Vancouver. But once the quiet of distance and solitude set in, something I did not expect to happen happened.

I cried. Every night for a month. Not from homesickness, but from relief. Thirty-seven years of rage, resentment, and exhaustion, all of which seemed to sink soft and slow into the carpet of my dorm room floor. The feeling paralleled that of finally leaving a relationship that had made you feel consistently frightened and gaslit. The idea that I could organize an exhibition without applying for a government license and not worry about possible fines. The idea that I did not have to submit scripts to a government institution a month prior to performance to get the show a rating. The idea of having discourse in a country where sex between men was not a literal crime, where raping one's wife was, where critiquing religious institutions would not put you at risk of breaking the law, where I could see myself, as a queer person, represented in local media.

The illusion of freedom that being an international student gave me did not last long. Three months into my journey, I came across a tweet from Travel Canada:

> Custom officers can request a drug test at point of entry into #Singapore. If you test positive for drugs, you can be arrested and prosecuted, even if the drugs were consumed prior to your arrival . . .

What the tweet did not say was that this applies only to Singapore citizens, workers, permanent residents . . . and not tourists. The Central Narcotics Bureau states that if you are a citizen or PR and are found to have "abused controlled drugs" overseas, you will be treated as though you had taken them in Singapore. Even if consumption is legal in the country you are returning from.

In other words, the stronger your legal status of belonging, the more likely you are to get punished for this particular crime.

It felt like, despite being eight thousand miles away, my body was still being treated as though it was state property. Like I did not need to live under the city's roof in order to be bound to its rules. Singapore, often criticized for its paternalistic style of governing, was, in true form, the ultimate parent.

I closed the browser window, imagining Singapore's children scattered across the globe, googling drug trivia and timing their returns. Trying to ascertain how long it takes drugs to leave the body.

———————————•———————————

The first time I had an at-length conversation about what it meant to leave Singapore, it was with Clara, a Singaporean I met in Vancouver. She had left Singapore almost a decade prior.

We talked about how hard it is to explain what it is like having fear coded into your national DNA. How the programming runs so deep that you don't even realize how governed you are by it till you leave. She mentioned how frightening it is to have any critique of the country published online. How aware she is that her family still lives there—how she worries about writing anything that would make it dangerous for her to return for a visit.

"I've been here so long and I still feel it," she said. "I keep thinking it's almost like a trauma reaction . . . but can I really say that? I mean, it's not like I've been through any *actual* trauma."

We broke eye contact and fell silent. We stayed that way for a while till she asked another question—one that brings up a whole other sort of sadness.

"Is there *anything* at all you miss?"

I don't miss much, but what I do miss, I miss a lot.

My favorite *nasi lemak* stall. The woman who runs it, her beautiful *tudung*s and her kind face, pair of tongs in one hand, banana-leaf-shaped plate in the other. Her "What you want, *sayang*?" The taste of that *nasi* mixed with *sambal*. The sweet shorthand of Singlish, every expression of which fills an empty place in my heart. The intimacy of never having to explain that which is untranslatable. The fact that I never feel as articulate as I do when I code-switch between the "proper" English I was taught in class and at home and the Singlish I learned everywhere else. That I'm never as funny without it. That I'm never as eloquent with my anger without it. That even if I spoke Singlish to my Canadian friends, and even if they understood, the lack of reciprocity would always feel like a wall.

And for all my griping about leaving because of people, people are what I miss most.

In 2018, I logged on to Facebook to see the copresident of Sayoni, one of the few organizations in Singapore dedicated to the rights and welfare of queer women, speaking into a mic in front of a backdrop that said "Repeal 377a!" It was a live video. The camera scanned the audience, which was peppered with people I know. For the first time since leaving, I felt tangibly homesick. I ached not being part of an event I knew I would definitely have attended had I been there. It felt not only like all the years I'd been vocal about queer rights were now irrelevant but also like I would not have the right to celebrate any change that did come. Leaving suddenly felt not only cowardly but also irresponsible.

All the years I'd spent living with housing precarity, I never felt alone. And I think that that is what kept me alive. Every time I was in emotional or financial trouble, someone was at my door with food or comfort.

Right up till the day I left, my community was there for me. Three months before I was to depart, the money that was supposed to support me through school had not come. I had three digits in my bank account, my school fees were due, and a client had told me that pending payment would be delayed.

When I posted my woes on Facebook, I started getting calls and emails. Someone offered to lend me money for the flight. Someone else offered what she called "bridge money." Someone set me up with a friend to help me with housing.

I got here on the dime of the very community I left behind. And even though I've paid all of it back, I still feel guilty.

———————◆———————

Singaporean poet Simon Tay claims that for those of us who cannot learn to love Singapore, there is no other city.

I've come to terms with the fact that I might never feel fully at home no matter where I go.

Canada is far from perfect, and I'm carving out what it means for me to live ethically as a settler here. But there isn't a day I don't worry about how long I'll be able to stay, or about everyone I love and have left.

Leaving personal and professional networks I took two decades to build feels brave. Leaving for my own happiness, not so much.

I wonder how long it takes guilt to leave the body.

———◆———

Rereading "Disneyland with the Death Penalty" in 2023, I still bristle with indignation at the tone of the piece and all the assumptions that underpin it. But this time, very begrudgingly, I am also struck by one of Gibson's speculations—one that wonders whether the lack of police presence in public space suggests that people in Singapore have, to quote William Burroughs, "the policeman inside."

It brings to mind a recent meme I came across on Facebook, circulated by Singaporeans. It contains four photos—the first three, labeled "USA," "UK," and "China," all depict different kinds of CCTV cameras. The fourth image, labeled "Singapore,"depicts a woman leaning out the window of what appears to be a high-rise, looking down at what is happening below. While I believe the juxtaposition was meant to be funny—a depiction of the archetypical *kaypoh* auntie—I am haunted by the other implication that seems to go unnoticed: Who needs CCTV cameras when we already excel at policing one another?

What does solidarity look like in a society of eat-or-be-eaten? In a country where one person's undoing is another's civic duty? At what point does fear stop being a reason for silence and start being an excuse?

When the monster eats your neighbor for lunch, are you as culpable for your inaction as the people who led it to the door? Who does it eat for dinner when it returns for you and finds your house empty?

When I think of activist friends who have risked so much more than I have with their actions, I am haunted by what James Baldwin once wrote about how civilizations are not necessarily destroyed by the wicked, but by the spineless: Is that what I am?

I ask myself if that makes me a monster.

I wonder how long it takes fear to leave the body.

Every night, I listen for knocking at my door.

If my self is a shadow, at least I made a dent in the light.

—Cyril Wong, "If . . . Else"

Letter to My Mother

I want to start with a cliché. To ask how long it has been. To scan the apartment—comment on what has not changed, ask questions about what has. To muse about how time flies, how death has a way of smoothing over the rough edges of life, the sharp, pointed corners of broken relationships.

But I can't. Because I know *exactly* how long it has been. The last time I was here, it was 2003. You were in your bedroom, working. Gramps was taking a nap. Nana was in the living room, watching television. This is the amber memory of my last day here, frozen for a decade and a half. I left, and three of you were here. Today, everyone is gone, and I return the same way I left—alone.

Do you remember my leaving? Did you see through all my stealth? I could not afford to move out all at once, so I packed whatever would fit into three plastic bags each day and transferred all of it to my new place after work. Three was the magical number. Small enough not to warrant suspicion—substantial enough for someone who did not own much. By the end of the week, I had moved everything I needed. The next day, I just did not come home.

Did you ever wonder where I'd gone?

I have so many questions about your apartment. About the objects it houses. As with most people who've lived in one place for many years, life does not change as much as accumulate. Closets brimming with clothes—all yours. Leftover medication from the cancer. Electronics thick with rust, carpets fat with the corpses of dead, unidentifiable bugs, books jacketed with years of dust, pamphlets concerning single parenthood and how to bring your child back to Christ.

Fifteen years we were lost to one another. Perhaps in another life, we are making up. Perhaps in another life, I had no reason to leave. Perhaps I know the names of all these strangers pressed between the pages of the twenty-five photo albums I am lugging home. Perhaps I knew my father.

I must admit, as I pillage your belongings, I think about how they might become useful to me: Maybe I will make drawings from these photographs. Maybe these documents can be turned into poems. Maybe all these personal belongings will become an installation piece called *Archiving Family*.

Archives are very popular these days with artists, you know. Very hip. Very *now*.

If I sound cold, it is because I am. The minute I understood my trauma had currency, you stopped being my mother and started being material. This icy attitude is how I survived. The day you allowed your church friends to exorcise the "lesbian demons" from my child body, you broke my heart in the process, so don't blame me for its malfunctioning, for this wintery ability to milk you for all you are worth. Make no mistake—you made me this way.

Packing up your apartment has really been the mildest part of this logistical nightmare. Thanks to your death, I have also been thrust headlong into a wonderful world of bureaucracy: conveyance lawyers, letters of administration, contracts, agents, knowledge about taxes. Off and on, I find myself feeling like a child. Like these are matters I should have knowledge about but don't. In these moments, I realize how sneaky Singapore is, how its culture of uniformity finds its way into one's flesh, embodies itself in how we think. Surely, there is no one way to be an adult. When I left you, I learned to eat three meals a day for under five dollars. I hacked the rental market and survived. I found my own family, wrote about it, carved a career from loss. Surely, this sort of adulthood deserves recognition too.

One of the last things I find in your apartment, I find on the final day of cleanup: a bright orange noose made from plastic rope, measured and looped, placed together with illustrated measurements, pushed to the back of Gramps's bottom drawer. It has been carefully double-bagged, and as I unpack it, I expect to find some random purchase Gramps made and forgot about. Instead, I come upon this object—an intention so deliberately crafted, it causes all the hairs on the back of my neck to stand.

I know what I am looking at when I stumble upon it but am unable to process it as real. My reflexive response is that I am having some sort of nervous breakdown. *Finally,* I think. All the feelings I thought I never had about my father hanging himself are materializing in some sort of psychotic break.

It is only when I find the suicide note, written the year Nana died, unopened till now, that I understand the noose was never used—Gramps had kept it as a safety net.

Taking out the last of the garbage, I think to myself that maybe I've been wrong all these years, that maybe I *did* inherit some of this family's genetic traits. After all, there were many times in my life that I wanted to die. Many periods I fantasized about it constantly. It was not a dramatic desire that announced its presence in loud sobs or melodramatic love songs. It grew slowly, quietly. A strong wanting for the inevitable to come quickly—tiredness the weight of bricks. These thoughts were the most prevalent the years I was living hand-to-mouth, waiting every other month for the power to be cut, moving house repeatedly because the rent had doubled or the lease was over or the landlord just did not want me there anymore.

Did you ever feel that way—too tired with life to see it as more than a chore? Those feelings, they don't go away. I've learned to master mine. To set them aside, acknowledge their presence, turn my back to their murmurings.

Did you ever read about the two young women who jumped from a flat in Toa Payoh? One was twenty-one, the other thirty. I read they were a couple. The news reached only the tabloids; they appropriated the tragedy as scandal, focusing on who had "gone to therapy," who had been "torn between boy and girl," how the younger woman had defied her parents.

Their bodies were found clad in red—a message to anyone fluent in local Chinese superstition: if you died by suicide dressed in red, it meant that you intended to return for revenge.

They also had red string tied around their fingers, arguably symbolizing a desire to be together in the next life.

I remember weeping when I read the article, feeling oddly complicit, oddly guilty. What had we done as a society to these two women, that even their love for each other could not undo? I hadn't known either of them, but I saw myself in their deaths. I saw their bodies as mine, their rage as my own. I wept over the act but took strength in the message: *This isn't the last you'll see of us.*

A friend once told me that anger and disappointment were two sides of the same coin—she said that anger was disappointment in disguise. Anger is bigger, louder, a force that pushes outward.

Disappointment runs deeper, closer to collapse, to the parts of us that are soft, vulnerable.

I've learned to hone my anger like a knife. I carry it around for self-defense. My anger at you, at this homophobic country. My anger at how so many queer friends of mine, born less middle-class, more gender-nonconforming, darker-skinned, have had it even worse, were thrust into the world with even less luck to weaponize.

I'm not sure why I bring all this up now. Why I am talking to walls. Why I am talking to you, the ghost of the woman I hated so much that the first thing I said when I heard she was dying was "Good. I hope it's slow, and I hope it hurts."

Those words, so final. Not just for you, but also for me: Is this really what I've become?

Perhaps this rage needs to die with you. No point, after all, stabbing at air. And shouldn't I be happy coming back to this apartment, this windfall that solves all the problems caused by my leaving it?

I should be glad that you no longer haunt me, that your specter exists only in photographs, in the minds of your few remaining friends. I should be glad that all you are is ash.

There is just one problem with letting the anger go—what to do with all that remains.

What of this disappointment settling in my bones? This house that failed at becoming home. These cracked tiles, this peeling paint, wind whistling through these windows.

What of this disappointment? These clothes left out to dry. This unfinished book. That broken lamp. This child you leave behind.

SOURCES

One Size Fits Small

AWARE on Body Image. Association of Women for Action & Research, 2010. https://www.aware.org.sg/wp-content/uploads/AWAREonBodyImageUpdatedSept2010.pdf.

"Aware: Women's Action." *Women's Action*, Association of Women for Action & Research, 2015. https://www.womensaction.sg/article/reproductive.

Goh, Gerome. "PSA: Appearing Naked in Public View Is Illegal, Even if You Do It at Home." SingaporeLegalAdvice.com, March 18, 2022. https://singaporelegaladvice.com/appearing-naked-in-public-view/.

"In Quotes: Lee Kuan Yew." BBC News, March 22, 2015. https://www.bbc.com/news/world-asia-31582842.

Lee, H. Y., et al. "Anorexia Nervosa in Singapore: An Eight-Year Retrospective Study." *Singapore Medical Journal*, 2005. http://www.smj.org.sg/sites/default/files/4606/4606a1.pdf.

Lim, Tin Seng. "Two-Child Policy." *Infopedia*, 2016. https://eresources.nlb.gov.sg/infopedia/articles/SIP_2016-11-09_103740.html.

Rowlands, Sam. "The Use of Forced Sterilisation as a Key Component of Population Policy: Comparative Case Studies of China, India, Puerto Rico and Singapore." *Sage Journals*, 2022. https://journals.sagepub.com/doi/full/10.1177/00195561221082984.

I Had a Dream I Was Your Hero

Wong, Cyril. "Father Figure." Facebook, 2016. https://www.facebook.com/notes/2704203236492533/.

I Hope We Shine On

Levy, M. S. "A Helpful Way to Conceptualize and Understand Reenactments." *Journal of Psychotherapy Practice and Research*, U.S. National Library of Medicine, 1998. https://www.ncbi.nlm.nih.gov/pmc/articles/PMC3330499/.

Stein, Alexandra. *Terror, Love and Brainwashing Attachment in Cults and Totalitarian Systems*. Routledge, 2016.

Becoming Monsters

Balmain, Colette. *Introduction to Japanese Horror Film*. Edinburgh University Press, 2014.

———. "It's Alive: Disorderly and Dangerous Hair in Japanese Horror Cinema." *Academia.edu*, delivered in 2008 at Perspectives on Evil and Human Wickedness. www.academia.edu/706281/It_s_Alive_Disorderly_and_dangerous_hair_in _Japanese_Horror_Cinema.

Looks Like the Real Thing

Awang, Nabilah, and Pei Ting Wong. "The Big Read: As Maids Become a Necessity for Many Families, Festering Societal Issues Could Come to the Fore." *Today*, November 2, 2017. https://www.todayonline.com/big-read/big-read -hiring-maids-no-longer-luxury-longstanding-issues-could-snowball-if -unchecked.

Cheow, Sue-Ann. "Numbers up and ages down for child suicides: experts explain." *The New Paper*, May 30, 2018. https://tnp.straitstimes.com/news/singapore /numbers-and-ages-down-child-suicides-experts-explain

Gardens by the Bay. "Unwavering Wonder: Annual Report 2020/2021." 2021. https://www.gardensbythebay.com.sg/en/about-us/about-the-gardens /annual-reports.html.

Goh, Raymond. "Singapore Tombstones Epigraphic Materials 新加坡墓碑铭集录."

Han, Kirsten. "Land-Starved Singapore Exhumes Its Cemeteries to Build Roads and Malls." *The Guardian*, August 7, 2015. https://www.theguardian.com /cities/2015/aug/07/land-starved-singapore-exhumes-its-cemeteries-to -build-roads-and-malls.

———. "Singapore: The Fight to Save Bukit Brown." *Diplomat*, October 30, 2013. https://thediplomat.com/2013/10/singapore-the-fight-to-save-bukit-brown/.

Heng, Janice. "Century-Old Olive Tree in Gardens by the Bay Bears Flowers and Fruits." *Straits Times*, September 12, 2016. https://www.straitstimes.com /singapore/environment/century-old-olive-tree-in-gardens-by-the-bay -bears-flowers-and-fruits.

"How Much Do Construction Workers Get Paid in Singapore?" *ColeBuild SG*, July 7, 2022. https://www.colebuild.sg/post/construction-worker-salary-singapore.

Huiwen, Ng. "Sungei Rd Vendors Receive More Help." *Straits Times*, June 16, 2017. https://www.straitstimes.com/singapore/sungei-rd-vendors-receive-more -help.

Humanitarian Organization for Migration Economics. "Extend Wage Increases for Cleaners to Migrant Workers." *Home*, August 18, 2022. https://www.home .org.sg/letters-to-the-press/2021/6/15/extend-wage-increases-for-cleaners -to-migrant-workers.

Hussain, Zarina. "How Lee Kuan Yew Engineered Singapore's Economic Miracle." *BBC News*, March 24, 2015. https://www.bbc.com/news/business-32028693.

Kapadia, Naeem. "One Metre Square: Voices from Sungei Road." *One Metre Square: Voices from Sungei Road*, blogger, August 20, 2019. http://crystalwords.blogspot.com/2018/07/one-metre-square-voices-from-sungei-road.html.

Koh, Raphael. "In the Twilight Hours of Sungei Road Thieves Market." *Coconuts*. https://coconuts.co/singapore/features/twilight-hours-sungei-road-thieves-market/.

Koh, Wan Ting. "Singapore the Fifth Most Expensive City Globally, Cars Cost the Most Globally: Report." *Yahoo! News*, June 16, 2022. https://nz.news.yahoo.com/singapore-fifth-most-expensive-city-cars-cost-report-052750837.html.

Leow, Joanne. "'This is Singapore' on Watching *Westworld* in the Diaspora." *Evergreen Review*, July 2020. https://evergreenreview.com/read/this-is-singapore-on-watching-westworld-in-the-diaspora/

Lim, Jun. "An (UN)Dying Flea Market?: Contesting State-Led Closure of Sungei Road Hawking Zone in Singapore." *Urban Asia*, December 14, 2020. https://urbanasia.blog/2019/11/20/an-undying-flea-market-contesting-state-led-closure-of%E2%80%A8-sungei-road-hawking-zone-in-singapore.

"Marina Bay Sands Net Revenue Up 107.6% in Q2." *Focus Asia Pacific*, July 21, 2022. https://focusgn.com/asia-pacific/marina-bay-sands-net-revenue-up-107-6-in-q2.

Milman, Oliver. "The price of life in Singapore, city of rules: 'It's a Faustian deal.'" *The Guardian*, January 5, 2015. https://www.theguardian.com/cities/2015/jan/05/the-price-of-life-in-singapore-city-of-rules-its-a-faustian-deal.

Ministry of Manpower Singapore. "Is There a Prescribed Minimum Wage for Migrant Workers in Singapore?" https://www.mom.gov.sg/faq/work-permit-for-foreign-worker/is-there-a-prescribed-minimum-wage-for-foreign-workers-in-singapore.

Nature Society (Singapore). "Public Walk at Bukit Brown Cemetery." 2012. https://www.nss.org.sg/special_announcement.aspx?id=c0%2FJTgZ6AKA.

RedTaurus. "Images of Old Singapore: Street Scenes @ the Shoppes at Marina Bay Sands." YouTube, June 14, 2015. https://www.youtube.com/watch?v=JZgb7GodzR0.

"*Singapore Tombstones Epigraphic Materials* 新加坡墓碑铭集录." Blogger, January 1, 2023. https://tombs.bukitbrown.org/.

"This Is How Huge It Costs for Gardens by the Bay to Keep Operating." *Singapore Business Review*, June 3, 2021. https://sbr.com.sg/leisure-entertainment/news/how-huge-it-costs-gardens-bay-keep-operating.

Ting, Wong Pei. "The Big Read: Singapore's Endless Love Affair with Private Tuition Just Got Deeper with Covid-19." Channel NewsAsia, August 6, 2021. https://www.channelnewsasia.com/singapore/singapore-tuition-centre-teachers-parents-students-education-2114136.

Youjin, Low. "Closure of Sungei Road Market: One Loyal Customer's Lament." *TODAY*, Singapore Press Holdings, 2017. https://www.todayonline.com/singapore/closure-sungei-road-market-one-loyal-customers-lament.

"新加坡 - 一览最新本地新闻." *8world*, June 22, 2022. https://www.8world.com /singapore.

Black Boxes & Penguin Pulp

"Adam Lambert Makes History as the First Openly Gay Male Artist to Top Album Charts." *HuffPost*, February 2, 2016. https://www.huffpost.com/entry/adam -lambert-trespassing-chart-debut_n_1539564.

Auto, Hermes. "Full Parliamentary Speech by PM Lee Hsien Loong in 2007 on Section 377A." *Straits Times*, September 7, 2018. https://www.straitstimes .com/politics/full-parliamentary-speech-by-pm-lee-hsien-loong-in-2007 -on-section-377a.

Blair, Olivia. "People Are Trying to Ban Adam Lambert from Performing in Singapore." *Independent*, December 1, 2015. https://www.independent.co.uk/news /people/petition-to-stop-adam-lambert-performing-in-singapore-over -promotion-of-lgbt-rights-gets-20-000-signatures-a6753491.html.

Cascone, Sarah. "Singapore Bans Gay Penguin Picture Book." *Artnet News*, July 14, 2014. https://news.artnet.com/art-world/singapore-bans-gay-penguin-picture -book-60556.

Chia, Adeline. "Why the Arts Cannot Flourish in Singapore." 2007. http:// mrwangsaysso.blogspot.com/2007/03/why-arts-cannot-flourish-in -singapore.html.

Chua, Alfred. "NLB Decision Guided by Community Norms: Yaacob." *Today*, July 11, 2014. https://www.todayonline.com/singapore/nlb-decision-guided -community-norms-yaacob?fb_comment_id=625878190858694_6262152508 24988.

———. "NLB Pulls Two Children's Books That 'Don't Promote Family Values.'" *Today*, July 9, 2014. https://www.todayonline.com/singapore/nlb-pulls-two -childrens-books-dont-promote-family-values.

Hickey, Shane. "Singapore Libraries to Destroy Copies of Gay Penguin Book." *The Guardian*, September 20, 2017. https://www.theguardian.com/world/2014 /jul/12/singapore-libraries-pull-gay-penguin-book.

Kolesnikov-Jessop, Sonia. "MDA Fines MediaCorp for Gay Scene." *Hollywood Reporter*, February 18, 2011. https://www.hollywoodreporter.com/business /business-news/mda-fines-mediacorp-gay-scene-110218/.

Lee, Joey. "This Guy Calls Rainbow Cakes 'Gay Cakes'—Are We Really in 2017?" *AsiaOne*, June 3, 2017. https://www.asiaone.com/singapore/guy-calls-rainbow -cakes-gay-cakes-are-we-really-2017.

Liyan, Mahmdiya. "Becoming a 'Singapore Girl.'" YouTube, June 26, 2016. https:// www.youtube.com/watch?v=P8U7MQXjztQ.

Martin, Mayo. "S'pore Writers Not Happy over NLB Controversy." *Today*, July 11, 2014. https://www.todayonline.com/blogs/forartssake/spore-writers-not -happy-over-nlb-controversy.

Philemon, Jewel. "Fear of Writing: A Commentary on Political Art and

Censorship." *Online Citizen Asia*, September 1, 2011. https://www.the onlinecitizen.com/2011/09/01/fear-of-writing-a-commentary-on-political -art-and-censorship.

Siau, Ming En. " 'Disappointed' MP Criticises HPB for Its FAQ on Sexuality." *Today*, February 7, 2014. https://www.todayonline.com/singapore/disappointed -mp-criticises-hpb-its-faq-sexuality.

"Singapore Censors Fine Cable TV Operator S$10,000 for AD Featuring Lesbian Kiss." *Gay News Asia*, April 10, 2008. https://www.fridae.asia/gay -news/2008/04/10/2040.singapore-censors-fine-cable-tv-operator-s-10000 -for-ad-featuring-lesbian-kiss.

"Singapore Fines Cable Firm for AD with Lesbian Kiss." Reuters, April 9, 2008. https://www.reuters.com/article/oukoe-uk-singapore-media-idUKSIN250 73620080409.

Tan, Roy. "Brother Cane." *Singapore LGBT Encyclopaedia Wiki*. https://the -singapore-lgbt-encyclopaedia.fandom.com/wiki/Brother_Cane.

Tan, Tarn How. "Fear of Writing." Epigram Books. 2012.

Wong, Cyril. "Not a Closure, but Who Can Say." Facebook, 2014. https://www.face book.com/notes/334769414422849/.

Yap, Melody. "Tips on How to Prepare for Sia Cabin Crew Interview." *Ladyironchef*, February 23, 2015. https://www.ladyironchef.com/2014/10/singapore-airlines -cabin-crew-interview/.

Where Are You From?

"Artists On Permits ft Singapore." Facebook. https://www.facebook.com /groups/227280455154593/.

Beech, Hannah. "Singapore Seemed to Have Coronavirus Under Control, Until Cases Doubled." *New York Times*, June 23, 2020. https://nyti.ms/33YKc9i.

Brutus, Bianca. "Jon M. Chu Regrets Characters' Depictions in 'Crazy Rich Asians.' " NBCNews.com. June 11, 2021. https://www.nbcnews.com/news /asian-america/jon-m-chu-regrets-stereotypical-casting-crazy-rich-asians -rcna1140?fbclid=IwAR3WeYuQpV3gWQrJt3bigkc5aqrbK3vMknWpifYvTfzTA OYRcjFwCbQ2TCg.

Cai, Weiyi, and K. K. Rebecca Lai. "Packed with Migrant Workers, Dormitories Fuel Coronavirus in Singapore." *New York Times*, June 11, 2020. https://nyti .ms/3fWPsNc.

"Coronavirus: In Singapore, Foreign Workers Were Locked in Dorm Room." *South China Morning Post*, April 23, 2020. https://www.scmp.com/news /asia/southeast-asia/article/3081005/singapore-foreign-workers-who-had -contact-coronavirus.

Farrell, C. "Judicial Caning in Singapore, Malaysia and Brunei." *Corporal Punishment Research*. https://www.corpun.com/singfeat.htm.

"Gov.sg: PM Lee the Covid-19 Situation in Singapore (12 Mar)." Gov.sg, 2020. https://bit.ly/33YKOf2.

Han, Kirsten. "Crazy Rich Asians Is a Win for Asian Americans, but It Gets Singapore Wrong." Vox, August 17, 2018. https://www.vox.com/first-person/2018/8/17/17715124/crazy-rich-asians-movie-singapore.

———. "Singapore's Migrant Workers Struggle to Get Paid." CNN, February 25, 2018. https://cnn.it/3am8kEd.

"HDB Ethnic Integration Policy (1989)." SG101. https://www.sg101.gov.sg/social-national-identity/examples/hdb.

Lotta, Edoardo. "Two Singaporean Siblings Published a Viral Video Questioning Chinese Privilege: They Were Investigated by Police." Vice, September 26, 2019. https://www.vice.com/en/article/8xw8zg/preetipls-subhas-viral-video-racism-chinese-privilege-interview.

Louis, Evelyn Teresa. "Religious Harmony in Singapore." *Massey Research Online*, 1998. https://mro.massey.ac.nz/bitstream/handle/10179/2423/02_whole.pdf?sequence=1%26isAllowed=y.

Malay, Michael. "Buy a Discount Maid at Singapore's Malls." *Al Jazeera*: "Business and Economy," June 27, 2014. https://www.aljazeera.com/features/2014/6/27/buy-a-discount-maid-at-singapores-malls.

Marsh, Nick. "Singapore Migrant Workers Are Still Living in Covid Lockdown." BBC News, September 24, 2021. https://www.bbc.com/news/world-asia-58580337.

Ministry of Foreign Affairs. "Moh Press Release—13 March 2020." www.mfa.gov.sg/Overseas-Mission/Berlin/Announcement/MOH-Press-Release—13-March-2020#:~:text=Border%20restrictions,-7.&text=a.,Singapore%2C%20or%20transit%20through%20Singapore. Accessed 1 June 2023.

Ministry of Health. "Pandemic Readiness and Response Plan for Influenza and Other Acute Respiratory Diseases." April 2014. https://www.moh.gov.sg/docs/librariesprovider5/diseases-updates/interim-pandemic-plan-public-ver-_april-2014.pdf.

Mokhtar, Faris, and Ishika Mookerjee. "Virus News: Luxury Hotels for Singaporeans in Quarantine." Bloomberg.com. March 28, 2020. https://bloom.bg/3oUn6if.

"MP Put on Blast for Saying 'It Takes a Virus' to Clear Field of Foreign Workers." *Coconuts*, April 7, 2020. https://coconuts.co/singapore/news/mp-put-on-blast-for-saying-it-takes-a-virus-to-clear-field-of-foreign-workers/.

Pappas, Stephanie. "Zombies Would Wipe Out Humans in Less Than 100 Days." LiveScience, January 6, 2017. https://www.livescience.com/57407-zombie-apocalypse-would-

"Prisons in Singapore." *Prison Insider,* 2017. https://www.prison-insider.com/countryprofile/prisons-singapore?s=les-liens-avec-l-exterieur#les-liens-avec-l- exterieur.

Ratcliffe, Rebecca. "Singapore's Cramped Migrant Worker Dorms Hide Covid-19 Surge Risk." *The Guardian*, July 1, 2020. https://bit.ly/3ao47j5.

———. " 'We're in a Prison': Singapore's Migrant Workers Suffer as Covid-19 Surges

Back." *The Guardian*, July 1, 2020. https://www.theguardian.com/world/2020/apr/23/singapore-million-migrant-workers-suffer-as-covid-19-surges-back.

"Sedition Act (Chapter 290) (Original Enactment: M Ordinance 14 of 1948." Singapore Statutes Online. https://sso.agc.gov.sg/Act-Rev/SA1948/Published/20130831?DocDate=19870330.

"Singapore Reports 407 New Covid-19 Cases; One Imported, 9 in the Community." *Channel News Asia*. https://bit.ly/2PRx7GB.

Smith, Tara C. "Zombie Infections: Epidemiology, Treatment, and Prevention." *British Medical Journal*, December 14, 2015. https://www.bmj.com/content/351/bmj.h6423.

Tan, Jerrine. "Asian Male Sexuality, the Money-Phallus, and Why Asian Americans Need to Stop Calling Crazy Rich . . ." *Medium*, September 3, 2018. https://medium.com/@jerrinetan/asian-male-sexuality-the-money-phallus-and-why-asian-americans-need-to-stop-calling-crazy-rich-e296abb77231.

Telling, Oliver. "Migrant Workers Suffer in Singapore's Hidden Lockdown." *Financial Times*, June 6, 2022. https://www.ft.com/content/4c63dea0-9ebd-4170-b978-5dceoc5e7f99.

Velayutham, Selvaraj. "Everyday Racism in Singapore." SpringerLink, Palgrave Macmillan UK, 2009. https://link.springer.com/chapter/10.1057/9780230244474-14.

Thin Line

Wright, Stephen, and Paul Bracchi. "'I'm Scared . . . the Skin Normally Tears After Three Strokes': Ex-Westminster Public Schoolboy Caught Dealing Drugs in Singapore Opens Up in His First Interview Since Learning He'll Be Strapped Naked to a Frame and Caned 24 Times." *Daily Mail*, January 18, 2019. https://www.dailymail.co.uk/news/article-6608935/Ex-Westminster-public-schoolboy-strapped-naked-frame-caned-24-times.html.

Yeung, Jessie, and Isaac Yee. "Tens of Thousands of Singapore's Migrant Workers Are Infected: The Rest Are Stuck in Their Dorms as the Country Opens Up." CNN, May 15, 2020. https://cnn.it/31SIVoL.

Dinner on Monster Island

Gibson, William. "Disneyland with the Death Penalty." *Wired*, April 1, 1993. https://www.wired.com/1993/04/gibson-2/.

"Government Subjects News Websites to Licencing Requirement." Reporters Without Borders, May 30, 2013. https://rsf.org/en/government-subjects-news-websites-licencing-requirement.

Han, Kirsten. "Singapore's Anti-Foreign Interference Bill Is (More) Bad News." We, The Citizens, September 15, 2021. https://www.wethecitizens.net/singapores-anti-foreign-interference-bill-is-more-bad-news/.

Heinsch, M., et al. "Death Sentencing by Zoom: An Actor-Network Theory Analysis." *Sage Journals*, 2021. https://journals.sagepub.com/doi/10.1177/1037969X20966147.

"MDA Clarifies Online News Licensing Scheme amid Criticism." *Yahoo! News*. May 31, 2013. https://sg.news.yahoo.com/mda-clarifies-online-news-licensing-scheme-amid-criticism-031829941.html. Accessed June 12, 2023.

"Sentencing and Arbitrary Detention of Mr. Seelan Palay." World Organisation Against Torture (OMCT), October 9, 2018. https://www.omct.org/en/resources/urgent-interventions/sentencing-and-arbitrary-detention-of-mr-seelan-palay.

"Singapore Is Cracking Down on Foreign Political Interference." *Economist*, October 23, 2021. https://www.economist.com/asia/2021/10/23/singapore-is-cracking-down-on-foreign-political-interference.

Stober, Eric. "Travelling to Singapore? You May Be Drug Tested for Cannabis, Travel Canada Warns—National." *Global News*, November 1, 2018. https://globalnews.ca/news/4616086/singapore-cannabis-travel-drug-test/.

Tay, Simon. "5." Department of English Language and Literature, National University of Singapore, 1985.

ACKNOWLEDGMENTS

There Will Be Salvation Yet was first published in Issue 28 of the *New Ohio Review* (2020), republished in *Queer Southeast Asia* (2021) and in *Making Kin: An Ecofeminist Anthology of Essays by Women Writers in Singapore* (Ethos Books, 2021).

Letter to My Mother was first published in *Journal—Centre for Stories* (Australia, 2020) and subsequently republished in *Letter to My Mother* (Marshall & Cavendish, Singapore, 2021).

Thank you for the use of your words:

The Body Is a Temple by Worms Virk first appeared in *New Singapore Poetries*, edited by Marylyn Tan and Jee Leong Koh (Gaudy Boy, 2022).

Fat Shame by Joel Tan was first published by the Substation (2017).

Alfian Sa'at's words are his own modified take on a line from his play *Fugitives*, produced by Drama Box (2002).

Too Many by Pooja Nansi first appeared in *The Straits Times* column Rhyme and Reason (2016).

"Handle with Scare" by Michaela Therese was released as part of her album *My Name is MEEKELLAH* (produced by Michaela Therese and Tim De Cotta, coproduced by Kelvin A., 2014).

If . . . Else by Cyril Wong first appeared in *Like a Seed with Its Singular Purpose* (Firstfruits Publications, 2006).

With thanks to . . .

The whole team at HarperCollins. With particular thanks to my editors, Adenike Olanrewaju and Sarah Ried. So much appreciation for the time, talent, skill, and care you have lavished on this book.

My agent, Amanda Orozco, without whom I'd still be floundering about on my laptop and crying into my manuscript.

My professors at UBC. With particular thanks to Kevin Chong, Sarah Leavitt, and Taylor Brown-Evans, who read some of these essays while the writing was still in various states of undress and whose guidance and insight were invaluable.

Ivan Coyote, whose kind and generous feedback to the earliest written essay in this collection made me believe it could be expanded into a book.

So many classmates who were early readers of several of these pieces, and so many fellow writers who tuned in on Zoom every Friday for two and a half years to write together in silence as a pandemic changed all our lives.

RR, whose comment about feeding the monster at lunchtime and having it come back for you at dinner helped concretize the soul of this book.

Cyril Wong, whose poised and consistent resistance is my perpetual inspiration.

Thea Lim, whose wise voice I kept in my head throughout the publishing process.

Napatsi Folger, whose love, laughter, and memes carried me through my MFA and beyond, and Marian Churchland, whose quiet, magical presence turns difficult work into parallel play.

So many activists still in Singapore, whose tireless work toward justice humbles me.

My beloved family: Michaela Therese, Jaclyn Chan, Robin Rheaume, Corinna Lim, Lisa Li, Vernie Oliveiro, Jack Porter. Thank you for your love and for your belief in me, and for keeping me alive.

And for my Platypus: thank you for the past decade.

ABOUT THE AUTHOR

Tania De Rozario is a writer and visual artist. She is the author of four books and is a Lambda Literary Award finalist. Her work has won prizes from the *New Ohio Review*, *The Comstock Review*, and Singapore's Golden Point Awards. Born in Singapore, she now lives and works on the traditional unceded territories of the Musqueam, Squamish, and Tsleil-Waututh First Nations, colonially known as Vancouver, Canada.